Tea With Douglas

Douglas Jeal is a working sculptor engaged in ways in which we communicate ideas through the exploration of light, place, colour and form.

In this book, written in collaboration with writer and designer Linda Rushby, he talks about his life and a career which has taken him from post-war Croydon, via St Martin's College of Art in Sixties London, to a long teaching career at Anglia Ruskin University in Cambridge. En route, he has travelled throughout Europe, the USA and Mexico, converted a disused church in the Lincolnshire Fens, been a Fulbright Scholar, contributed to the debate on public art and met many of the luminaries of late 20th century art.

A natural raconteur, his stories, sometimes hilarious and sometimes heart-breaking, describe his experiences as one of the first generation of working class students exposed to the 'Art School' scene; capture the atmosphere and excitement of making art in the second half of the 20th century and beyond; and give a fascinating insight into the creative process.

www.douglasjeal.com

Damson Tree

Damson Tree is an independent company offering editing
and design services to authors who wish to self-publish
www.damson-tree.co.uk

Tea With Douglas

Conversations on art and life

Douglas Jeal and Linda Rushby

Damson Tree Publishing
April 2014

ISBN: 978-0-9929048-0-7
Copyright © 2014 Douglas Jeal and Linda Rushby
Designed, typeset and published by Damson Tree Publishing, England
Typeset in Adobe Caslon Pro 11(13.2)pt
www.damson-tree.co.uk

Contents

Foreword by the Editor

I first met the sculptor Douglas Jeal in the summer of 2010 in Bury St Edmunds, Suffolk, at the private showing of an exhibition by one of his ex-students, Susi Gutierrez. He was due to retire from lecturing at Anglia Ruskin University in Cambridge in 2011, and wanted a website to form an archive of his work over a career that stretched back to St Martin's College of Art in 1960s London, and beyond that to Art School in post-war Croydon. He liked the website I'd made for Susi, and he asked me to take it on.

Before we started work, he broke his leg in an accident and was taken into hospital, then was housebound for a while. At the time I was going to a breakfast networking meeting in Cambridge on alternate Wednesday mornings, and I started visiting him after my meetings. We would go over the text and images that he wanted to include in the website and discuss progress, then drink tea and eat toasted teacakes while we chatted and he told me stories from his life as an artist and a man, funny, sad, shocking, amazing, hilarious, heartbreaking stories.

As the website took shape and the time came for it to go live, I knew I was going to miss our Wednesday mornings. I was looking out for a book project to launch my publishing venture, and one day I asked him:

'Have you ever thought about writing your memoirs?'

I bought a voice recorder, and our alternate Wednesday mornings continued through the summer and autumn of 2011, whenever both of us could make it. The first few interviews took place out in his garden, with songbirds in the background. I would switch on the machine and get him to talk, which was never much of a challenge. Then I transcribed the interviews, a much bigger job than I realised at first. I tried using voice recognition software, but most of what it produced was gibberish. I persisted, thinking that it would learn to recognise Douglas's voice, I reduced the interviews to 10 minute chunks that would be easier for the machine to deal with, but in the end I discovered that it took me less time and effort (and was more interesting) just to play them back and type them myself.

We finished the last interviews, leading up to Douglas's accident and our starting work on the website, in January 2012. Shortly afterwards I went away travelling for six months, and the project went into suspension. On my return in August 2012, we met again and resumed our alternate Wednesdays. I finished the transcriptions and gave them to him to check, then began the job of going through them all, imposing some structure and chronology, checking dates, taking out the repetition, filling in the blanks, finding a way of expressing it all that read as a coherent story, rather than a conversation, but still retained Douglas's own voice.

This book is the outcome of that work, our joint efforts to capture a life in words.

Linda Rushby, Editor
Prague, Czech Republic, July 2013

Note: As editor, I have quoted direct speech in some places, where Douglas reported conversations in that way. Please note that this is done to support the flow of the narrative, and is not intended to imply that the original words have been quoted verbatim.

Chapter 1 - Early Life and School 1944-59

I was born in 1944 in Croydon, just outside London. My father was in the army, and he wasn't demobbed for a few years after the war ended, probably not until about 1949, so for the first bit of my life I lived with my grandmother in a council house, a terrace very similar to the one I'm living in now. Of course, they wouldn't have called themselves working class, they were lower middle class, and my grandmother was interested in all art. Like most families, my family had a lot of problems. I think my mother's schizophrenia was due to my grandmother's lack of love, because she really wanted a boy. She had actually had a boy, but it was stillborn, and I don't think she gave my mother much love.

My mother was an only child, and her father, my grandfather, was a Douglas, from the family of Black Douglases. His father came down from Scotland and made a chain of pastry shops along the south coast, Hastings, Brighton, Hove, and so they were quite middle class, lower middle class, and my grandmother came from Bow Road, so she was quite working class, but she had aspirations. She was the first person to think of me as an artist, and I remember drawing in her kitchen while she was doing the housework. I'd just be drawing with a crayon, and she would comment about how good it was. That was an early thing that I think inspired me to be an artist.

She had a collection of strange cosmetic boxes, a sort of rouge, in plastic, rectangular, shapes. They were made of a very beautiful dark blue plastic, almost ultramarine, but often the dyes were different. Fitted into that rectangle was a white lid with a cardboard thing to show you what shade of rouge it was, and she kept these just for me to play with. She had a whole collection of them in a drawer. You couldn't do anything with them because they'd got very soft rounded sides, but I loved the shapes and the colours and some of them were much more translucent. I think they had a huge influence on the sculptures I'm making now.

My grandmother came from quite a big family, there were lots of different children because her mother married four or six times in her life. I don't think she was ever divorced, so her husbands must have died on her. She went with an older man when she was young, and then married men who could support this family. I met my great-grandmother and she wasn't a very nice person in older age, in fact I was absolutely terrified of her as a kid, but that's the recollection of a young child. She was then married to her last husband, who was a really nice man. I can remember him, he seemed very soft and gentle. She dressed completely in black and had a very crooked nose, so to me she looked like an old witch. I could only have been about 5 or 6 just before she died, and I didn't like her at all. I don't think she and my grandmother got on, which is presumably why she left home early.

All the evidence I've got is that my grandmother must have left home to go and live with my grandfather at 15, in a place called Woodside near Croydon. I know the house they lived in because I've been there. It was a big Victorian house like the ones I lived in as a student. They both put down they were residing at the same place and the marriage certificate isn't for years later, so obviously they lived together before they got married. The more I looked into it and heard about other people's grandparents, I realised the 1940s were much more prudish than earlier decades. Underneath that Victorian thing, people did live together outside marriage, and that was quite common I think, for people who wanted to get away from the family situation.

My grandmother was a self taught young woman who really wanted to better herself, a very self-motivated East Ender from Bow. She didn't have an East End accent, she spoke, not posh, but really good English and she just wanted to have a different sort of lifestyle than the background she came from. She was very cultured, she taught herself lots of things including French, and she was gifted creatively. She played the piano, I remember she had a lot of sheet music, Chopin and Liszt, and she also played the zither and the mandolin.

Both my grandfathers were in the First World War, my dad's father I believe was in the trenches, and my mum's father, because he was a pastry cook, was in the supply, so he was just behind the trenches. He used to tell me stories, like once when he had to go up to the trenches for something and they gave him a white tent. It took him two days to get there and when he had travelled all this way he unpacked his rucksack to sleep and he'd got a white tent and he said, how bloody stupid, because they had planes and balloons, it was very frightening. He was a sitting target but it was so cold outside he decided to sleep in the tent and take the chance.

I don't know how it came about, but after the war finished he was offered a job looking after the war cemeteries in Normandy or Picardy and so my grandmother went with him and they lived in Normandy somewhere near Lille. They lived with a French family which I suppose was good because they would have picked up a lot of French. They were both self-taught in French and somewhere I've got both of their dictionaries, First World War dictionaries, because the soldiers were issued with French dictionaries. One of them has a stamp on it saying 'Ministry of Defence' or something.

So she had this cultural sense and obviously they'd gone to Paris. They were quite aware when they came back, of the Charleston and so on, they used to go dancing and she'd got these beautiful dresses which I don't think my mother kept when she died. She lived into her seventies and she had these beautiful Charleston dresses from the 1920s hanging up in the wardrobe.

My grandmother was quite a collector, and I had things from her, like a Moroccan octagonal table and her mandolin. I don't know what happened to the zither, it could have been buried with her because I know they buried one of her musical instruments with her. Because they only had one child, my mother, and they both used to work, she had a bit of pocket money and she used to go round the so-called antique-cum-junk shops. It was that time in the 1940s, when people really didn't care about antiques, they weren't as expensive as they are now. She would buy all sorts of things, some of which I've inherited, there were others that got lost along the way, in particular a Greek vase and a Tang vase. She had plants as well, I can remember, you went into the hallway and there was a particular Victorian plant, an aspidistra, in a purple pot and she had lots of art objects. She gave my mother two quite important porcelain vases with cupids going round them which I think were worth quite a lot of money, but my mother being my mother broke them. Although she was their daughter she put no value on creative things at all, very strange, they took her to museums and she didn't react at all.

My grandmother had a relative who was in the navy, either a second cousin or a relation of my grandfather, I don't know which, and he used to bring her things back from Japan and places. A lot of them I can remember were just turned out for the tourists, but she did have other things like a Tang vase from China, I don't know where she picked that up from, whether it was an antique shop, I don't think he would have brought it back because I think I saw most of the stuff he brought back for her, nice stuff but really just tourist souvenirs. She had a mixture of tastes, a lot of the stuff she collected was quite modern but at the same time mixed with Victorian things. She used to tell me stories about going to the Crystal Palace, which must have been when they came back from France.

That was the background to my education in the arts, and of course she used to take me to museums - the Horniman's Museum which was in Forest Hill in London and to the Victoria and Albert and so on. The British Museum was an eye-opener for me, it wasn't the British Museum we know now, all the showcases were just packed full, there was no design but it was incredibly valuable for me as a 15, 16-year-old student to see that because they had a lot more on show in those days than they do now. Most of the stuff is down in the vault and some other places. Most of those museums, including the Tate, have vast quantities of stuff that's never shown.

So my grandmother was, I suppose, the first person to encourage me to make art. Then when I went to school there was a teacher called Miss Branscombe and she set us all, at the age of 5, to do a head in plasticine, and I did one of a pirate, and she went ecstatic over it. She then got us to put linseed oil on the plasticine, and then paper maché over it. I remember waiting for this thing to dry on the school radiator and then cutting it up, taking the plasticine out and sealing it up again. For some hideous reason I painted it with bright orange poster paint, with black eyebrows and hair and a black moustache and eye patch. Then because the whole idea was for it to be a hand puppet, my grandmother made a dress for it.

Miss Branscombe was so enthralled by this puppet that she said, without a shadow of a doubt, it was the best thing in the room. Until then I didn't realise I was capable of anything like that, I didn't have any confidence at all as a child and I was always getting beaten up when I went to get my jacket from the cloakroom, because I had very curly hair and looked rather effeminate. My grandmother used to say to me 'You should have been a girl', which is funny in a way because of her attitude towards my mother, who she wanted to be a boy. I suppose that's why she put all the energy into me, and most probably there was a bit of jealousy in my mother's attitude towards me.

Miss Branscombe then brought me in this block of salt, the sort that you give to animals, cows and so forth, on a farm, to lick, and she said: 'Look, here's a knife, carve that' and that was the first carving I did. That really set me up for a career in art, at the age of 5, it came quite early. Before I went to secondary school I was doing pictures of crucifixions. It's quite interesting, because I would do them as designs for stained glass, not paintings in themselves, it was mainly to do with relationships of colour and shape.

That's how I was started on the road to being confident about myself as a creative person, because I come from a background where the only confidence I got was from my grandmother. When I stopped living with her, that was a nightmare, because my mother had no interest in me whatsoever, and yet she used to tell me all her woes, she was constantly ill, or she thought she was. My father used to come home at six or half past six and expect me to be in bed, so there was no real contact there, except in the holidays, and he was very critical of everything I did. He would always pick out the things that were wrong. I suppose, although I didn't realise it at the time, as a 5, 6, 7-year-old, I really did miss the environment of my grandparents' home, because that was completely different. My grandfather was a really nice man too, and when I went there he tried to get me to read and helped me, but there was none of that at home, we didn't even have a book in the house. We had no television, no books, we had a radio that was worked by liquid batteries, which looked like an aquarium turned upside down, with liquid in it, acid of some sort.

The saving grace was my cousin, Derek, who was quite a lot older than me. He was called up for his national service and chose to go in the RAF. He came to see us on a regular basis, generally once a week. I don't know why he was attracted to my father, but he used to come and see me. A lot of my cousins used to come and see me, I had another elder cousin called Jackie, who's still alive, who actually went to art school before me. Her father, although he was my father's brother, was much more into art and music than my father. She used to come and see me, and when I was in my early teens she used to take me ice skating, but this older cousin, Derek, who was in the air force, showed me how to shape balsa wood and make model aircraft. I started going to the Cubs, but I felt completely out of place, because I was the only working class boy there, all the others came from middle class backgrounds. I felt really out of it, they didn't want to know me, they didn't try very hard, we had to work for badges, and I had no co-ordination so I couldn't catch a ball or stuff like that, and yet I was incredibly good with my hands.

I remember once when I was about 8 or 9 I think, on one of the weekends when I didn't stay with my grandmother, I went with my parents to see my other grandmother who lived about 15 minutes from my mum's mum, and we called in on my mum's mum on the way back. My parents knocked on the door and there was no answer and I looked through the letterbox. All the inside doors were open, and knowing my grandmother, having lived with her, I knew that wasn't right, so I said to my father 'this is strange because she's gone out and left all the inside doors open, that's not like Granny at all'. Anyway he didn't take any notice and what transpired is she'd gone down as she always did on a Sunday, to meet my grandfather when he finished work about three o'clock in the afternoon. She used to go and meet him half way, and I used to accompany her when I lived there, we used to have a walk together.

Somebody had obviously known that she did this every Sunday, so they broke in, they went in through a small window in the bathroom, and then they completely ransacked the place. I saw it the day after, the police came, and it was a tip, it was awful what they'd done. I'll never forget it, they'd just taken out all the drawers and turned them upside down, ripped up the carpets looking for money. It was absolutely mindless, they'd done stupid things like they'd turned a vase full of flowers upside down so the water went everywhere, and they'd ripped the seats of the chair with a knife. After that she moved, which was a real pity but she said 'I can't live there any more' it was like being raped, you know, like being violated. The thieves got away with about a thousand pounds they had stashed under the carpet, so I don't know whether one of them said something to some neighbour or something, but it was rather stupid of them. They got away with quite a lot really, and they were only after money, I don't think they took anything else and there were quite a few antiques which they didn't take. So I think from that, I learnt a lesson then to lock doors and things. I didn't think of people stealing my sculpture for scrap though, but that's another story.

I went to quite a nice secondary modern school because I couldn't read and write, they'd call it 'dyslexic' now, but at that time they just said you were backward. I think I was in the second lowest or lowest class when I started, but I worked my way up into the top class before I left. The great thing about it was there were some really good, enthusiastic teachers there, who spent a lot of time with me. The school didn't really want to know me after I left except when they saw my name in the paper, and then they sent me a letter saying: 'We're having a reunion'.

There was one boy, Peter Bennett, who was at primary school with me and went on to the same secondary school. I suppose we were similar in intelligence because we seemed to stay in the same class all the way through primary and junior school. When we got to secondary school, we were in different classes, so we didn't see each other that much in the class itself but we saw each other at play time and of course we used to hang out together because he was the only person who'd gone to that secondary school from my primary and junior school so we were quite friendly especially when we first got there because we hadn't made that many other friends.

Peter's parents gave him a bicycle because he lived further away from the school than I did, whereas my parents wouldn't allow me to have a bicycle, I don't know why, either they couldn't afford to buy me one or they just didn't go along with children riding bicycles. I did get one much later because I worked on a paper round and bought myself one.

I remember one day in December, I'm not sure whether I was 12 or 13, but it was very dark, I was walking home from school and Peter was cycling the route that I walked, he just had further to go. We'd got to a bridge in Croydon called Windmill Bridge, it was a bridge over the railway but at the top there was another road coming in from the left. Peter had just struggled to get up the hill and somehow he overbalanced and a lorry was coming up the other road, and the lorry was just about to stop, because it had to give way, when Peter fell underneath the front wheel which crushed his head.

By the time I got there the workmen were lifting the lorry and getting him out and I just remember seeing him lying there with blood completely covering his head. It hadn't squashed his head so much I suppose as it was just a very bad fracture, but it killed him. His head wasn't actually squashed, I remember that, it was still intact but it was all cracked and bloody.

There are a lot of different things that I remember about that and it certainly did shape me and has shaped me for the rest of my life, I think. The first thing was I looked up and I saw this workman looking at me and he took his overcoat off and laid it over Peter's head so I couldn't see it and Peter's feet stuck out. I'm not sure if this is accurate but I could have sworn that he was wearing sandals with socks, and I know in the summer he wore the same type of sandals as my sister, although she was a lot younger, she was only 4 at the time, but it was the same sort of standard style of sandals that you could get anywhere. So for some reason I rushed home to see if she was okay, it was just the way my mind worked. But nobody was at home at all and after about an hour my mother came in with my sister and said 'I hear a friend of yours died on Windmill Bridge'. She didn't say anything else to me, she must have known that I knew him, she must have met him, but anyway she didn't say anything.

The three of us went off to the market as we always did on a Friday night, and one of the worst things, I think, more than seeing him, was actually seeing in the market his elder brother, David, and his father, looking for their mother in the market to tell her, they obviously knew, and that really did stick in my mind, that awful feeling - I felt so much pity for them.

But of course, in those days, nobody asked me if I'd seen it, I wasn't asked to be a witness, nobody took any notice of me I suppose, maybe because I didn't hang around, I went off to see if my sister was okay. My mother wasn't interested whether I'd seen it or not, she never asked, although she knew I came over the same bridge, and so I think I just bottled it up, until I was at the Tavistock Institute when I was 28, 29. But just talking about it still affects me, I'm still emotional about it.

It's a very strange thing for a child to see. And it was just like - I remember a child telling me 'Father Christmas doesn't exist, it's just your parents' and you suddenly feel really let down and your whole world of that fiction disappears. I feel now, looking back, that's what happened to me, suddenly I was conscious of death, and I'd never been conscious of death before, and that really did change me I think, from then on I came to be a bit of a manic depressive. When I was having therapy at the Tavistock Clinic and we looked back, it was then that I started getting the symptoms of being neurotic and depressive.

I've thought about him a lot over the years. Often with crises in my life, I've ended up making a sculpture about them and that somehow has erased it. When I was young I had pneumonia and I used to have this recurring dream of rectangular white shapes going away from me, and every time I was ill I would still have the same recurring dream, the two things were linked, illness and this dream. But when I was at St Martin's I made a white sculpture which was based on it, and once I'd made that sculpture it sort of exorcised it and I didn't have the dream any more.

But I've always thought Peter's death was far too powerful for me to comment on and I wouldn't know how to do it, it's nothing to do with the forms of the bicycle, or the lorry, it was to do with his death and also my psychological shake-up. For the first time I really realised we're not immortal, and at 12 or 13 that's quite a shock. God knows how people in the third world deal with it, but I suppose in our society, where death isn't portrayed very much at all, it's a shock when it hits you. On Spanish television, they show you people dead in car accidents, and I'm sure children see it on the Spanish television, but we don't do things like that in this country.

I think I just blotted it out at the time, after he died. I know it was almost into the Christmas holidays, I think it was about 13th December on a Friday and it was dark, that was the other thing, it was quite dark because it gets dark about four o'clock at that time of year. I think the whole episode just disappeared and I never really thought about it again. I didn't even think about him, missing him, it was only much later, since I've got older, that I've thought about him and wondered what he would be like, all the questions people ask themselves if they lose a child or a friend, I wonder what he would have grown into being. I can still remember his voice and everything, which is very strange, because if you asked me about other friends of that time I couldn't do that, but in my head I can still remember his voice and how he used to speak and it's rather strange. I suppose the brain retains an incredible amount of information. I don't think it affected my work directly, but it affected me and I think it led to my being a manic depressive.

My mother was always a little bit mentally ill, she was classified as a schizophrenic, and when I was 12, she was put into a mental hospital because she was frightened of killing me. I remember being called to the headmaster's office, the welfare people were there, and they asked me, how many times did she hit me, what did she hit me with, and that was quite horrendous for me. I didn't know what to say, because if you've lived with a schizophrenic mother all your life you're used to it, that's the only person you really know. Although of course in my case that's not completely true, because I lived with my grandmother the first five years of my life, so I did have an alternative mother figure. But I suppose I just shook it off, and didn't really pay too much attention to my mother, expecting her to be how she was.

But after that the school really did change to me, they took much more interest in what I did, and I suppose the plus for me was that I got out of a lot of academic subjects, and they realised that I was good at art. I got called in and the art teacher said I'd just been commended in a drawing competition, at the age of 12, from all the schools in Croydon. It was a charcoal drawing of the railway lines where I lived, and he obviously spoke up for me and that was when they suggested I go to the art school, so they got me into doing Saturday mornings at the art school which you could do if you were that young

The other members of staff at the secondary school got me making things too, I did all the posters for the school fête, I did big drawings of knights in armour for the history teacher, to go on his classroom walls, I did all sorts of things. So I spent most of my time drawing. And I suppose some of them weren't too nice to me, but most of them were.

Chapter 2 - Croydon School of Art 1959-62

While I was still at secondary school, I started going to the Croydon School of Art on Saturday mornings. At that time it was in a beautiful Victorian house, in a big park with stables at the back where they used to serve tea, and a big conservatory which was designed by Joseph Paxton who designed the Crystal Palace. I don't think it was designed as a school, because of the stables. At 11 o'clock in the morning and 3 o'clock in the afternoon we used to break for tea and biscuits in the stables along with the staff. I noticed when I came to Cambridge that Fred Hoyle, at the Institute of Astronomy, used to make a big thing that everybody should break at 11 o'clock in the morning and 3 in the afternoon, and they did the same at Croydon, that was a great thing, which I really miss.

I think that is where my love of collecting plants started, as well as from my grandmother. Art schools were quite full of plants, because of the importance placed on drawing as the basis of art education, and at Croydon they had a big array of plants, especially the sort of plants that the Victorians brought over like cheese plants and begonias, because of the beautiful conservatory, very cold in the winter and very hot in the summer.

When I was 15, I left the secondary school without an O-level to my name, I hadn't got anything, because in those days you could leave at 15 and you didn't have to have O-levels to go to art school, if you were good you went. As soon as I got into the art school full time, they moved it to the local Technical College, which was a hideous building, from about 1936, which looked as though it was designed by Speer and the Nazis, as if it had come out of that era of totalitarian state architecture. It's still standing, so I must be careful what I say. That was a shame, because we didn't have our 11 o'clock tea, we had to have it up in the refectory with all the other students. But that was okay, we did mix with the other students, they were doing all sorts of things from day release, whatever a technical college did in those days.

It was quite a change from the park to the middle of Croydon. There were lots of different types of people, there were maybe four or five working class boys and most of them were doing graphics. In fact, I started off in graphics because that was what my father wanted me to do. He wanted me to earn a living as a graphic designer, but I was pretty useless at it. It was called our 'craft', the craft was your specialisation. It was like a foundation degree course, you got a bit of everything, but at the same time the craft was the thing you did one day a week, and the rest of the week was made up of a lot of drawing.

The whole idea of the art schools in Victorian times, based on the Arts and Crafts movement, was that drawing was the most important part of your art education. So when I was at Croydon we had three days a week of drawing: plant drawing, life drawing and then often we went out to do some sort of observational drawing. That was the core, and because of that the art schools were full of plaster casts which you had to draw, and when I was a 15-year-old boy first at art school I had to draw these awful boring plaster casts of the Venus de Milo and other classical figures. It's not as exciting as drawing a real model for obvious reasons, the way the light falls on them is so different from the way that light falls on a real person because a real person is quite sort of satin and the light is reflected in the curves, where with those casts somehow everything gets deadened by the chalky plaster surface. So it's very strange trying to draw plaster casts compared to real human beings, but of course we were too young at that time to have a real-life model. But it was the Victorians' thing that of course they were quite prudish so that plaster cast drawing was the discipline, and also drawing plants. I liked all the drawing, life drawing, plant drawing, outside drawing which I really enjoyed, though I wasn't so keen on the life drawing, but I think that was the lecturer, he spent most of his time chatting up the young women students.

When I got interested in really getting down to do work, the staff were really good, like at the secondary school. There was a woman called Mrs Holden who was an incredible teacher for pen and ink drawing, and I did some nice drawings with her, some of which I've still got. She got us to do a lot of plant drawing in pen and I enjoyed that. I saw her again a few years ago, I noticed she was drawing at the Cenotaph in London. Then I did so many weeks at ceramics, which I did enjoy. I didn't make pots, I made ceramic sculpture and painted it. I didn't like painting very much, I don't think I was very good at painting. I'd realised quite early on that there were a lot of people much better at painting than me.

I had a teacher called Dennis Piper, who also taught at St Martin's, but he taught graphics to me at Croydon. He liked me and I got on well with him. He was quite a cool character, he was very tall and had this sort of stance, like Samuel Beckett, he wore desert boots all the time, with a suede coat, you could tell he used to concentrate on looking cool, and he was an absolute jazz fanatic. He said to me 'God, you're a messy worker'. In those days, we had to write all the Baskerville and Gill Sans etc and then paint them all in, and I could never keep to the lines, I always smudged it. I was a messy worker, there's no doubt about it, and this was my one day a week craft specialisation.

Then I did sculpture, and they had a guy called Mark Clarke, who was taught by Dobson at the Royal College of Art. Frank Dobson was a really good ceramic figurative sculptor between the wars, and Mark got me interested in Frank Dobson's figurative sculpture, which I was influenced by and by Henry Moore. Mark Clarke sort of took me under his wing and he said 'You're good at sculpture, you ought to do sculpture'. So it was then, within the first nine months of being full time, that I changed from graphics to sculpture with Mark Clarke and a young woman constructivist sculptor who taught me on Fridays. He also got me to enter sculpture competitions, of which I won two, and this gave me a bit of money and it also gave me a lot of prestige in Croydon, my name was in the local paper.

Of course, my father wasn't very happy about me giving up graphics for sculpture, and that was about the time that I moved out. A friend of mine,

Fred Carver, who was a painter, was living in a big Victorian house, and he said, 'well, move in with me, I've got room in my room', so that's what I did. I must have been about fifteen or sixteen. My mother never forgave me, she said: 'I saw you come down with your friend' because we literally carried my bed with the bed clothes on it, up the road all the way to this Victorian house, about two or three miles. I think the rent was about 25 shillings (£1.25) or something like that. I don't know how I paid for that, I'm not too sure whether my father paid for it. I got a grant from the local authority to go to art school, because my father didn't earn very much, and he used to give me pocket money so he most probably paid my rent out of that.

So then I was on the road to being a sculptor, and I had to go and tell Dennis Piper, who taught me graphics, that I wasn't going to do it. I think he was quite pleased, and a couple of years later I met him at St Martin's. It was a different situation in those days, with art school. A lot of the lecturers were older than the students, some of them were very old, but others were young, like Dennis Piper, who would have been in his late twenties. So we socialised more with the staff, and of course, at St Martin's we mixed with the staff all the time, and a lot of the teaching actually was done in Mooney's pub on Cambridge Circus, after the official lectures had finished. It was a completely different attitude to teaching, much more camaraderie and all-in-it-together.

Going to art school changed me completely, because these older students who had done their National Service said to me: 'Have you read this, have you read that?' Suddenly I was confronted with Hemingway and Steinbeck and all these people, and Laurie Lee, 'Cider With Rosie', and I realised I enjoyed reading and I started to be quite an avid reader, because we didn't have television in the student house.

I made some good friends while I was there. One of them was David, who was quite an extraordinary person, he looked the same age as me but was actually six years older and had come from a completely different background. He'd been to a public school, I'm not quite sure which one, possibly it was Charterhouse, he'd then done a degree in architecture and after that he'd come to Croydon to do painting. He was quite a good painter, and we got on really well, we had some great fun together.

We went on holiday together, David and I and his girlfriend Hilary, to Brittany in an old Standard 8 convertible, a very nice old car, and that in itself had its adventures. In his earlier life David had gone out with a young French lady, and kept in touch with her. The three of us, David, Hilary and I, stayed in a field behind his former girlfriend's mother's *crêperie*. On the way from Dieppe I had my first experience of drinking cheap wine, and paid for it dearly. We arrived in the dark with it pouring down with rain, we were all absolutely soaking and we put up the tent. Then when we woke up in the morning we found we'd just pitched the tent on the cliff face, about three foot away from the edge!

On the way back, we were taking the Brittany to Dieppe road and we'd left it a bit late, so we were travelling through the night in the dark and suddenly we came to a village and there was a search-light in our faces, and a man standing there with a sub-machine gun. The French military were looking for Algerian terrorists and there was this great big thing in front with spikes on it, that would wreck the tyres if you didn't stop! Luckily the soldier just laughed when he saw us, most probably they knew we were English because of the old Standard 8, and we showed him our passports and went on our way.

There was another teacher at Croydon who taught me sculpture, called Peter Atkinson. He was very good, and he actually took me down into the technical department where the students came on day release from industry to learn how to weld and he taught me how to weld. He was also teaching at St Martin's and so it was on his suggestion that I apply to St Martin's.

He said to me 'There's a really good exhibition at a place called the Grabowski Gallery and it'll give you an idea of the sort of work the students are doing at St Martin's School of Art'. So I went along to see this exhibition. One of the people who was in the exhibition was called Maurice Agiss and he had some really nice sculptures in a combination of wood and stone so I thought 'yeah, well St Martin's seems to be the place for me' so I arranged an interview. Sir Anthony Caro, who was the Head of Sculpture at St Martin's, interviewed me and said 'Yes, you've got a place, come in September'. I also applied at that time to Bromley and got accepted by both places.

In the summer, before I started at St Martin's, I applied to work as a porter for British Railways, because they took on students at Victoria and my friends from Croydon worked there, so they put me on to it and it seemed like a good way of keeping in touch with them. But that first summer I worked there, they were all at Victoria, but I got sent to Battersea Park Station and it was horrible because I was the only student there. You had to have one of those funny flat caps and an arm band. There weren't many trains, I read a lot of novels. There was a Pakistani guy I worked with who was always disappearing, he would go to the pub and then come back and leave me to look after the trains. It was like something out of an early Alec Guinness film, the foreman just sat in his office drinking great big mugs of tea all day. They had a pot-bellied stove thing with the kettle on all the time. They never did any work, and the guards would come in and have a cup of tea. It was very informative about how British Railways staff worked.

We had to sweep the platforms. Battersea Park platform was made of wood and there was a lot of dust so I had to go out with a watering can and sprinkle it with water and then sweep up so you didn't get clouds of dust that would annoy the customers. They weren't worried about me but they were worried about the passengers. The other thing I had to do was clean the toilets early in the morning which I didn't like doing and especially the ladies', it was a bit of a shock. There was a school, I think it was a Catholic school, and these teenage girls always used to get off the train early in the morning, and go off to the Catholic school. The first time I had to clean the ladies' toilets over on that platform I got the biggest shock because I never imagined ladies' toilets to have really crude and rude graffiti in them, and people had thrown used toilet towels and things. It wasn't nice, I mean I expected it of a man's toilet but I didn't expect it of a woman's toilet at all, in fact at Battersea Park the graffiti in the women's toilet was worse than the graffiti in the men's, and a lot more of it I might add!

Chapter 3 - St Martin's College of Art 1962-65

I arrived at St Martin's in 1962. It was quite an eventful time, because Tony Caro interviewed me in the January before the new academic year in 1962, and when I got there, to get a grant I needed them to say that they'd accepted me, and being the sort of person I was then, it got all the way to September and they hadn't actually sent me anything in writing. So I arrived on the day to find out that they had no record of me at all. And the head of the Sculpture Department, Frank Martin, said to me, 'Well, Caro isn't here for me to ask', because Caro actually only taught one day a week, all the time I was there. Sometimes he came in for two, but he was a part-time teacher, he wasn't a full-time teacher. Virtually all the staff in the Sculpture Department were part-time, and Frank Martin, the head of it, was the only full-time member of staff.

Frank Martin said: 'Well, I'll put you on probation till Christmas and see how good you are, and then if you prove yourself creatively I'll give you a place'.

That left me in a bit of a quandary, because as far as I was concerned I thought I'd been accepted to St Martin's, and David, my painter friend from Croydon, had been accepted to Ealing Art School. So before the term started, we selected a point between Ealing and Central London, where I was going to be in Charing Cross Road, and we picked on Notting Hill Gate as this was roughly half way between the two of us to try and find a flat so that we could share digs. We managed to get a room in Westbourne Grove, run by a couple of Irish people who were very funny. Next door there was a young lady who was most probably on the game, because there were so many male callers, and it was a very interesting place. We both came from Surrey, so at weekends we both used to go home or go to stay with friends, we didn't want to stay in London to begin with. We'd already arranged this room, and I obviously had to pay my half of the rent, and I didn't have a grant, because I'd got nothing from St Martin's in writing, they wouldn't give me anything until the Christmas.

Another strange thing that happened was that I'd got to St Martin's because I'd won a competition for Ingram's Hearing Aids to do a sculpture, of all the students that put in for it, I won this competition and I made this piece of sculpture, which was cast, then another competition came up which was for Kenco coffee houses, they were just starting in England and they'd got coffee houses all over the place, and there was obviously one in Croydon, and I won that competition too, I did this 6ft by 2ft plaque called *The Musicians*, still got a photograph of it somewhere.

There I was in Notting Hill Gate and trying to decide what sort of job I was going to have to do so I could carry on going to St Martin's. I realised that it wouldn't be any good missing classes so I had to get something in the evening. The only place that would give me a job was Kenco Coffee Houses, and I had to wash down the kitchens of all the Kenco Coffee Houses which was an awful job. They were all in the basement, all incredibly hot, and my job was to clean all the pipes, for the Environmental Health inspections. It was horrendous, I used to start about eight o'clock at night and finish about twelve or two in the morning. I did it right up until the Christmas, and it was very strange, having won a sculpture competition and done a sculpture for one of their houses to be just a cleaner.

Caro in the mean time, had said, 'Oh yes, I do remember interviewing you' but he'd obviously forgotten to put me down, or some secretary or somebody had forgotten to do it. But I think it must have been recorded somewhere because I knew the starting date, so somebody must have sent me that information. Anyway, at the end of that autumn term they decided that I'd proved I was worthy of a place and they then wrote off to Croydon Education Authority and I managed to get a grant. And that pleased me because it was back-dated to September.

The flat was very strange – well, it wasn't a flat, it was just a room – and we decided to divide the room in two. There were a couple of chests of drawers and a wardrobe, and we each had a bed, so we put these things down the middle of the room and had a bed either side so we had a bit of privacy.

As I've said, David and I got on really well despite having very different backgrounds, and we had some great fun together. Notting Hill was full of a lot of Irish people then, and quite a lot of other groups. The Carnival hadn't started then, but it was an interesting place to live. And this particular house was good, though it was a very strange place. One day after we'd been there about six weeks, the landlady came up and knocked at our door, the Irish woman who owned it, and said: 'You always go away at the weekends, why don't you stay? We have a little get together in the basement on Saturday night' she said, 'You'd love it. Why don't you stay this week?'

David and I talked it over and decided, yes, it might be an idea to go and see. He'd broken up with his girlfriend so he was thinking, like I was, perhaps there'd be some young females.

Anyway, we went down into the basement, and there were drinks, there was music, but it was completely covered in pictures of Stalin. It was a communist affiliated party meeting, that's what they did down there, and they were trying to convert us. We only went the once, we couldn't take the dogma more than once, but it was quite interesting.

That first winter I spent at St Martin's, 1962/63, was a very hard, bitter winter. About Christmas time, all the pipes burst in the Notting Hill Gate flat and we had no water. David's idea was, because we were on the first floor, we could climb out of the window onto this flat roof which had another kitchen underneath. And he decided that we'd collect snow and boil it up, because we had no water, and make a cup of tea. When we boiled it up in a saucepan it was absolutely scummy and black. It was so funny that the snow looked white but when you boiled it up, it was awful, so we went out to some coffee bar for tea.

By the Christmas we had both decided to move back to Croydon, because it was too expensive for us living away in Notting Hill and also we didn't have the space we did at Croydon to work in vacation on our art works. It wasn't just the cost of the room, although we were paying quite a lot of money for it, about £10, about £5 each I think, which was quite a lot of money for 1962/63. We each had a room to ourselves in the Victorian house which we rented together in Croydon, because David was there too, and the rooms cost us 25 shillings each, so £1.25. That was a lot, lot cheaper, but then you've got the train fares, so we thought about it and totalled it up. It wasn't so bad for me, I could walk to East Croydon station in about 10-15 minutes, and then the train only took about 10-15 minutes to get to Victoria, and then all I had to do was catch the tube to Tottenham Court Road or Leicester Square. But David had to go all the way to Ealing, so he bought himself a motorbike and he used to set off every day. And we did that for the remainder of the three years that we were both there, we stayed in this beautiful Victorian house.

The Victorian house was very very big, with about four or five storeys, with a cellar as well, and servants' quarters half way up the stairs, a huge conservatory, an orchard and a huge lawn and a huge double garage at the bottom, which was big enough for two sets of coach and horses. It was a beautiful house, and it was ideal. We both had the conservatory which we used as a studio. So we did have fun, and there were other students there that we knew from Croydon.

And studying at St Martin's was really good. The first term was getting to know the place. I'd already done three years at Croydon, including over a year's sculpture, so I knew a lot about the history of sculpture and Caro was filling me in on much more contemporary sculpture. Tony Caro, Philip King, David Annesley and Mark Bolus were the main sculpture tutors and it was fun and it was very very friendly, and the first year passed quite easily I suppose. Mainly we had projects to do and it was a very post-graduate sort of environment. You were left to your own devices but you had individual tutorials.

And of course London was on the doorstep. The first thing I did, I already knew about the British Museum from Mark Clarke, the sculpture teacher who'd taught me at Croydon, and he'd got me to go to the British Museum and the Tate, what is now the Tate Britain. I was quite fond of the British

Museum and in those days all the collections were higgledy-piggledy, just jammed into glass cases, there wasn't this incredible one thing in a glass case that it is now. The African collection was amazing, just so many objects to look at, and the smell of the wax polish they used for the wooden cabinets. So when I got to St Martin's it was rather nice during the lunch break to pop off to the British Museum because it was only about ten minutes walk away and so I used to spend a lot of my lunchtimes there.

There was another student there who was doing sculpture, I can't remember his name, but he was also studying anthropology at London University. He was a nice guy, he'd already been in the RAF so he was a lot older than I was and he had a friend who worked in the British Museum. So he used to come into the sculpture department.

Mainly in the sculpture department there were rooms upstairs, and especially in the first year we weren't really allowed to go down into the welding rooms which were down in the basement. They were occupied by second and third year students so we had to do projects upstairs where there was a rather nice carving room. The carving teacher was much much older than the rest of them, he'd obviously been there for years, and I did a couple of boxwood carvings very simple like Brancusi I suppose, and then there was a sort of plaster room which was very small.

There was a yard out the back and by the time we'd got to Easter the next term I'd actually built myself a shed in the yard. I quite liked the isolation of being on my own and I did a lot of small maquettes there, the lecturers would come down and find me. So I spent a lot of the time outside once that bitter winter had disappeared and that was a very bitter winter, it went on and on and on. So within the first year we moved back to Croydon and were commuting. Sometimes it was a bit difficult because as I got to know the staff and the students there were a lot of things going on, lots of activities.

During the summer I went to work for British Railways again, and this time I was bright enough to phone them up and say 'I want to go to Victoria, not Battersea Park thank you very much'. I spent three months at Victoria, and that was an eye opener because that was a complete regime. You had the foreman in charge of the trains, and one porter with the foreman on each platform and the foreman has the times of the trains. And just before the train is to leave there's a button on the platform, a big round button on one of the pillars that support the roof, and he presses the button to tell the signal box that that train is ready to leave. And then when the green light goes you blow the whistle, lower the flag, and out goes the train. Most of the foremen were very good, and you were allowed to go off and 'fluff', which meant you went off with a little two-wheeled porter's barrow and caught the trains as they came in from the south coast, or any train, but mainly it was the big trains that came in, it wasn't the little trains that came from Catford or Lewisham or Croydon, somewhere like that, it was the ones from Brighton or Hastings. Mostly it was the Brighton trains because on the Brighton trains there would be well-known people who were coming up to act in the theatre or something, or they would have been on holiday, and of course then you went up to them, asked if they wanted a porter, put their luggage on, called a taxi for them, and then hopefully they gave you some money. And at the end of the day after doing all this we used to add it up and give the foreman so much money. Some foremen didn't ask for any money at all, they were very good, they realised we were students. Some of them did but they never asked for half or anything, you just gave them a contribution. During the weekend we used to make about 25 shillings a day (£1.25), which was quite a lot of money. And then of course we went and sat in the pub and drank it all!

It wasn't all rosy though, because you had to do shifts. The worst shift was six in the morning to two in the afternoon because you didn't get many people. You got some people coming up at eleven o'clock from the coast, if you were lucky, to see exhibitions and stuff, but mainly you were after people with luggage and they didn't come up at those times. So you didn't get 25s every day all the time. If you worked on the six o'clock the chances are you might have got assigned to cleaning out the toilets, you certainly would have got assigned to sweeping up before you went off and fluffed, so there wasn't much fluffing in the mornings. Then there was another shift from ten in the morning to six, that was quite a good shift to do, but you got all the manic people going home at five o'clock, the rush hour, and generally you had to be on the platform helping the foreman at those times. Then there were all-night shifts, you could do six to six or you could do ten to six. If you were lucky you ended up managing to find a train to sleep in about two o'clock in the morning, but you had to be careful the train didn't go out, a friend of mine ended up in Brighton! At that time there were some beautiful coaches, with beautiful lamps and stuff, and of course the Brighton Belle was still running then.

It was quite a good job, but it did have its limitations. There was one time when I was stuck on the platform with two trains and the foreman had just seen one train out and then he had to go somewhere – I forget where he had to go, but it was quite legitimate. The train went out and a man who had been saying goodbye to his girlfriend jumped out of the train at the end of the platform. There was a woman standing there waiting for another train and he hit her really hard and knocked her over. So I rushed off to see that, grabbed hold of the bloke because you're not allowed to jump off the train when it's started moving, and then a woman came up and told me that a man had just been taken ill on the other train on the other side of the platform. She didn't say how bad he was, and I was still trying to deal with the one who had jumped off and hit the other lady. I called the railway police and they came and took the first bloke away, but in the meantime the man on the other train died from a heart attack. It was one of those corridor trains, I think it was the London to Brighton train.

The ambulance came - there must have been someone else on the platform who called the ambulance, so it wasn't as though nothing had been done - but by the time I got back with the railway police the ambulance men were trying to get him out. They couldn't get the stretcher in, they can't get stretchers in and out of those railway coaches with the corridors, they had to manhandle him out. I don't know whether he was dead then or he died later but they had to manhandle him out and then put him on the stretcher. They had like a seat thing, if I remember, but it took them ages getting him out. So the job did have its traumas.

I'd saved up quite a bit of money from working there, I'd scraped together £50, and that was quite a lot of money for the 1960s, my Dad was probably earning only about £15-20 a week. I wanted to buy a vehicle, and somebody told me: 'You can buy a vehicle from the army' so I wrote to the Ministry of Defence people, and they sent me a catalogue. It was in a place called Ruddington in the Midlands, and I went up on the train, which was cheap in those days. I got sitting opposite this man with a check suit, he looked like a book-maker, but he was actually an agent who went up there and bought these Austin Champs and then did them up a bit and sold them in North London for £160 to people like myself, contemporary young men and women who wanted to drive around in something a bit different. He said: 'I'll help you if you want to come and have a look'. I was shocked because these Austin Champs were huge, big Jeep-type things, with a 2838cc Rolls Royce engine in them. They all were encased so that they could go under water, and had snorkels. And they were selling them at £5 each. Now the amount of brass on them, because all the electrical fittings were brass, the amount of brass on them you'd have got your money back just for selling the brass, even in those days. The agent chap said: 'You don't want one of them' because he said 'They've got nothing in them. If you want to sell it again to people like yourself, you want one that's kitted out with the shovels' and he said 'more than that, you want one that's got a proper canvas soft-top cover'.

We found one, and there was a person like myself bidding, and in the end it went up to £80 and I got it. I don't know if it was quite £80 or that's what it cost me altogether because I had to ship it back, because it had got army number plates so I couldn't put it on the road. Not only that, but I hadn't even passed my driving test yet.

I shipped it back to Croydon and my father came over to see it, because he was quite excited, Dad never was a dampener on anything, he was always interested in my ideas, and the only problem he said was: 'The trouble is son, if something goes wrong with this you've got this huge bill facing you to keep it on the road and because the engine is encased to keep the water out, you're never going to be able to do any repairs yourself, with this engine you wouldn't know where to start'.

He said: 'If I was you I'd sell it!' Those were his exact words. And I said: 'No, no'. Well, I couldn't take it out on the road, the insurance was costly. At the big Victorian house where I was living, the drive was enormous, so I tried it out on the drive. My father had been teaching me to drive in his Ford Anglia, which was quite different from this thing that weighed a couple of tons I should think, and what I didn't realise was the power of the thing. Although the brakes were good, a 2838cc engine is a huge engine and the acceleration was phenomenal.

Well, the first thing that happened, I put it in gear, and let out the hand brake, and that was okay, and I fiddled about with it, and I couldn't find reverse, because what you had was a gear stick with five gears, and then another gear stick to put all that in reverse, so you had five gears in reverse. So I suddenly realized what this other stick was, so I put it in reverse, put it in the wrong one – in second, I think – zoomed backwards, knocked down a young sapling and hit the gatepost. It was lucky I didn't end up on the pavement, because I was totally illegal – I'd taxed the vehicle, and insured it, and I'd got my British number plates by then, so it was all legal in that way, it was just that I didn't have a driving licence. I had a provisional driving licence, but that meant you had to have somebody with you. I was on private land on the drive, so that was okay, but it wouldn't have been if I'd gone outside. Well anyway, the way that tree went down, and the gate and the gatepost, ended up as matchsticks, I thought: 'I think I might think about selling it'.

We put the number plates on and my father came round, and my father used to be a driving instructor, in the war, he used to take recruits in tanks, he was posted both during the war and afterwards in Scotland, in Lanarkshire. So he took me out in it, and the first thing we realised was it only did 8 miles to the gallon. So I thought, right, I've got to get rid of it, so I looked in *Exchange and Mart*, and looked up this guy who I'd travelled up with on the train, because I knew what his business was, and he was selling them, with all the shovels and everything, for about £160 to £180. So I put an article in the paper, and the same day the paper came out I got a telephone call from a rather nice man. I don't know what he did, he was a lot older than me, I was 19, he was most probably in his late twenties early thirties. He had an aeroplane at Biggin Hill, and he wanted to tow it around from place to place. He thought the Champ was wonderful, and he gave me £160 for it, so I made £80 profit, I was a lot better at earning money in those days than I've been recently. I didn't buy a car with it, I bought materials as usual, I didn't buy clothes, I never really had much clothes. And then, maybe five or six years later, a friend of mine gave me a Volkswagen Caravette, and that stayed with me for some time, that was quite a good vehicle.

In the second year at St Martin's we were given a lot more autonomy. Quite early on Caro had an exhibition at the Whitechapel Gallery and he invited the students to the private view which was disastrous really because we got drunk and started having a disagreement with Anthony Armstrong-Jones about sculpture. I don't think Princess Margaret really said very much, I think I and one or two of my student friends said a bit too much to Anthony Armstrong-Jones.

We used to socialise with the staff a lot, much more than I've done with my students, and that was rather good. You learnt a lot by socialising. I used to go with David Annesley, one of the lecturers, to the Establishment club, which was just round the corner, and I saw Marcel Marceau there and I think I saw Dudley Moore and Peter Cook. I was quite fond of jazz at that time, Thelonius Monk and John Coltrane and people like that. I went to Ronnie Scott's and met Dennis Piper, who was my graphics teacher at Croydon, he was teaching at St Martin's as well. It was rather good arriving in a new art school and you knew some of the faces already. There were two lecturers there from Croydon, Dennis and Peter Atkins, who took over the job at Croydon after Mark Clarke left to become Head of Sculpture I think in Melbourne College, in Australia. Peter Atkins also taught at St Martin's, not sculpture, I don't know what he was teaching, but he used to give me really good critiques and he was a very good lecturer.

Then I met Bryan Robertson who was the director of the Whitechapel Art Gallery. I hadn't been to the Whitechapel before and they had quite a few contemporary exhibitions. So all in all it was quite a formative place and the second year was really good, again quite a bit of excitement.

About that time Michelangelo Antonioni was making a film called *Blow Up*, with David Hemmings as the lead character, playing a photographer. He was shooting at a night club in Oxford, and he got half way through shooting when the police raided it and shut it down. So then he managed to persuade Borehamwood studios to recreate this night club, got the Yardbirds – the group that was playing in the original film – back on stage, and he resisted the film unions from providing him with film extras, because he said, 'I don't want film extras, they don't look anything like the people that were down in the club'. Of course a lot of the people who were down in the club in the original shoot were from Oxford University, so he went round the art schools in London. I don't know how many he went to, but there were quite a lot of students there, so he must have gone to more than just St Martin's – perhaps to Central, Royal College of Art, other places. He met my girlfriend while he was at St Martin's and because he didn't have much time to come and see us he just said, 'Look, this is the sort of students I'm looking for, can you round me up some students?'

We didn't know what we were in for, we set out in my father's Ford, packed with people, and it was rather good really, because when we got there, we were told we were only needed for one day's shooting. They dressed us up, they dressed me in a top that looked like a Picasso top, you know, striped, French, blue and white. I was a different sort of person to what I am now, because I was very self conscious and I didn't like my photograph being taken, so I kept at the back, which was lucky really, because I believe all the camera work went over my head.

The first day's shoot, there were rumours that Antonioni was in bed with the leading lady, but I don't think that was the case, I can't remember who the leading lady was now, but anyway, he didn't turn up. Now that was quite good, because we were being paid £10 a day. Out of that £10 we had to pay 10 shillings (50p) to the union, because they were outraged that he wouldn't use their film extras, and also to cover the health and safety if one of the students were to be hurt on the set so we had to pay 10s to the union, but it still left us with £9 10s (£9.50) and the cost of getting there, which wouldn't have been 10s, so then we had the whole day to kill because we couldn't go home. We didn't know he wasn't going to be there, so we turned up at the allotted time, nine o'clock or whatever, and then he didn't come, and it got later and later, and they supplied us with coffee. I got talking with one or two of the cameramen and people and they said 'Have a look round, we'll call you'.

We had a look around Borehamwood Studios, and it certainly wasn't boring. There was an aircraft hangar with a huge water tank where they did the galleon models, and another aircraft hangar that was absolutely amazing, because we went in there, and there was a whole long table of women working on plastic models of spaceships, at least 10 or 20 different models being made. I realised later that that was probably *2001, a Space Odyssey,* they were already starting on that, because they looked like the sort of ships in *2001* when I went to see it. So that was really interesting to see the film industry and the stuff that was going into it.

We went back again the next day, and there was a problem with the Yardbirds' lead singer, he was supposed to break up a guitar and he cut his fingers doing it on the strings, so that meant another postponement. We were there three days altogether, which was really good because we were only told one day, and so we got £30, for something that was actually quite interesting to see. Michelangelo was quite an interesting chap, not that he talked to us, mind, he was just there on the set and you could see the way he was working.

So being in London was quite a different experience from being in Croydon, and that was quite a change from being at home between 15 and 16, to going to live in a Victorian house with a group of other students, most of them older, because they'd either come from public school, or they'd gone into National Service, or like myself from state school.

Anthony Caro as I've said was a huge driving force at St Martin's, although he actually only came in one day a week, he was a good teacher. Frank Martin was the Head of Sculpture and I have vivid memories of him, he always wore black: a black sports shirt, black trousers, black shoes and a black coat. He'd been in the army and he was rather a sergeant-major sort of character. He was a student of Dobson and out the back in the yard were a lot of life-size Dobson-type figures which actually belonged to Frank Martin, he just left them there, he wanted somewhere to put them. He lived in the Isle of Wight so he had to leave fairly early in the afternoon to get all the way back to the Isle of Wight every day. He was quite a character, he nearly threw me out a couple of times because of disagreements I'd had with staff.

Most of the sculpture teachers like Caro, David Annesley and Mike Bolus were all traditional metal sculptors. Philip King deviated a bit because he started using resin and things, but basically it was the same traditional format. Philip King done engineering at Cambridge and he organised a very good lecture by a physicist, and we were all enthralled by this, he was talking about 3 dimensional space, and breaking a ham sandwich up. We were all mesmerised by this because it did seem to fit into a sort of constructivist approach, deconstructing sculpture, the sort of first ideas about deconstructing stuff. There were other people who were brought in to give lectures, like Bernard Cohen, Gustav Metzger, Alexander Trocchi, Dick Smith and Jeremy Moon.

They brought in Bernard Cohen, who was a painter, to do a project on communication and I was too busy on my sculpture to bother with media communication so I really let rip that I thought it was a waste of my time. The trouble was I did it in front of all the other students, so I was hauled into the office and Frank said 'if you do that again you're out, I'm giving you fair warning, you don't do things like that'. So I had this view of Frank Martin that he was a bit of a pain in the neck, to me anyway. I knew he didn't like me, but Caro liked me and one or two of the people that came in liked me.

Jeremy Moon was one of them, he was a good painter, known nationally, he died quite young I think, in his 30s or 40s, some time ago, which was very sad because he was an interesting man, a good painter and I got on well with him. He liked me because we thought on the same plane, I used to do everything in my sketchbook first and so did he, he used to do drafts and things, and that's how I made my sculpture at the time when I was at St Martin's. I used to rough it out and put my ideas down and it was much more a process of making a piece of sculpture from an idea rather than, as I've done lately, making a piece of sculpture from what I'm doing with the material, the material might suggest something to me. But those two ideas have always gone hand in hand.

Gustav Metzger, the auto-destructive artist, was another one. I bumped into him again in Barcelona in 1999, and I saw him in Cambridge in January 2012. When we met in 2012 I asked him who was responsible for bringing in all these different people, and actually I was shocked to hear it was Frank Martin because I'd got this view of him as being very traditional so I misjudged that, misjudged him really.

It was quite interesting seeing Gustav again, and it was good to put it in context because although Caro was important to me there were these other people as well. Caro was there the whole three years that I was there, but people like Gustav and Alexander Trocchi and Jeremy Moon and people like that only just came in for one session but they still stick in my mind as offering something completely different.

The Bernard Cohen thing was quite interesting because I nearly got thrown out. I didn't do the project, I went back and did my own work, so I did risk getting thrown out, but I wasn't. The funny thing is, when I left St Martin's, I met Bernard at a private view and we were incredibly friendly, he didn't hold anything against me at all. I haven't seen him for about twenty years but every time we met we got on really well and I actually do like his paintings - it was just Frank and this sergeant-major type person that he was that I was rebelling against, but obviously he was very intelligent as well to bring all these different people in.

There were a number of painters that were an influence on me and Dick Smith was one, he was an up-and-coming artist then, and he did these three dimensional paintings that stuck out from the wall, I think he was quite an influence on me. Ellsworth Kelly was another, the American painter, of very simple shapes, so they were quite important for the first sculptures that I did after I left St Martin's, especially the one that the Museum of Łódź has, you can see that they're very simple shapes too. It's funny that in a way I was more interested in painting than sculpture, I was never really influenced that much by Caro, I did metal things but then I was making metal sculpture before I went to St Martin's. I'd already learnt about the Russian Constructivists when I was at Croydon, as well as Julio Gonzalez and Pablo Gargallo who were the first metal ferriers, wrought iron sculptors, who influenced both Caro and David Smith in America. There were lots of connections, but I already had those connections before I got to St Martin's, and actually I remember having the feeling when I got to St Martin's that they weren't really pushing me on much from what had happened at Croydon. But I can see that they did, because of these other people coming in, and I did actually like the teaching of Annesley and Bolus who were new to teaching, they were ex-students at St Martin's that Caro or Frank Martin had brought back.

I think students were much more rebellious in the 1960s and certainly I was. In St Martin's there was a lot I didn't go along with and I might have been a bit pretentious at that time too, you know 'I'm a sculptor and I just want to make my own work, I don't actually want to fit in to some pattern that is run by academia'. If you look at a lot of the great sculptors like Gaudier-Brzeska and Brancusi, they had exactly the same problem. I think you are actually being taught by who you meet and how you interpret that rather than formally. I assisted Caro during one holiday to weld up some of his sculptures, he did ask me a couple of times to weld things up and you learn a lot more about somebody's process by doing that. I wouldn't want to do it as a job because once you're in that technician role you're stuck in it. But you do learn a lot from watching the process at work.

I think that at best an institution can offer you an openness of mind and

Frank obviously was very good because although he was a bit dictatorial he also brought in other people that could offer different things. But the problem is he tried to enforce it, and because he was enforcing that everybody do this Bernard Cohen project I sort of rebelled against that and I was the one who voiced it most but I don't think I was the only one, it's just different personalities.

Before I went to St Martin's I had seen and heard about the Russian Constructivists because they were starting to appear in art magazines. Although they were around at the beginning of the twentieth century, it took a long time for them to really become well known in the west, I think there was only one book at the time written on the Russian Constructivists. Zwemmer's book shop in Charing Cross Road was a really good place to go, and they had different exhibitions and books or pamphlets on the Russian Constructivists so I got into those. I was very fond of Malevich's *White on White*, so there was quite an influence going on from the Russian Constructivists. I think it influenced us all, it wasn't just me, but Caro, everybody, the whole idea of taking sculpture off the base and putting it on the floor so it stood up in its own right, it wasn't something to stand and look up to, it could be lying on the floor, or whatever. There was a piece by Tatlin called *Corner Relief* that really influenced us all, it was a piece set in a corner and a lot's been written about that and different iconic kind of graphic images, Russian images.

By the time I got to the third year I'd decided to spend the whole year, my last year there, making this huge piece of sculpture which was based on Stravinsky's Rite of Spring. When I was living in the Victorian house at Croydon with David, his room always used to resonate with Stravinsky's *Rite of Spring*. I got rather attached to this record and although I already knew some classical music, like Shostakovich, I hadn't come across Stravinsky and Prokofiev, and so it was new ground .

My final year sculpture was quite a big piece, I think the circle was about 8 or 10ft in diameter, and it was about 15ft long. It was made out of aluminium and steel and it was a feat to get the piece to stand up, and at the same time I wanted a lot of movement in it echoing physically some of the movement in the *Rite of Spring*. It was a very colourful piece too, because it was made up of coloured plates.

That was my finishing exhibition, to have this up on the roof and to have the whole gallery to myself. I showed nearly all the pieces that I'd done there, including a white piece that I'd done in the second year, which was very much liked by the American critic Clement Greenberg when he came over, he said it was very minimal, because minimalism hadn't arrived from America then, Donald Judd, Robert Morris and people.

I put this thing up on the roof, because that was the only place we could get, the only space at St Martin's that was big enough for it. It had to be constructed in pieces and then it was bolted together. A friend of mine, John Groves, who had also been a student at Croydon with me, doing graphics, came up and photographed it for me because he was quite a good photographer. He'd just managed to get it done, when there was an incredible thunderstorm. We'd put it up on the roof, and unfortunately it was higher than the lightning conductor and the sculpture got struck. It was actually amazing the damage the lightning could do, it was a solid piece of metal over a quarter of an inch thick and it just split it. It was amazing that we weren't up there at the time.

I took it down and it never ever got reassembled again. For years I kept it but then it was too much to carry around, there was a hell of a lot of it to carry about. I've still got the circle somewhere, it's all I've got left, that and some slides of the complete piece.

Chapter 4 - Post St Martin's 1965-67

I was put forward for the Sainsbury Award when I left St Martin's. I think there were about four or five of us put forward by London art schools, there may have been other art schools from the rest of the country, I don't know. The award was divided between myself and Roland Piché and possibly one other person, I'm not sure, I've forgotten how much money it was. I think I got the Sainsbury award on the basis of the maquette for the very big sculpture I did in my final year, but I did show all the sculpture that I'd done in the three years I was at St Martin's. I exhibited my work down in the basement of the Tate, and I was amazed at going down there and setting up my work because there were just stacks and stacks and stacks of sculpture and paintings. There was tons of stuff down there, all beautifully stacked and it's the same with Saatchi and the British Museum, most of their stuff is in storage.

There were very few contemporary galleries in London at that time: Kasmin, who was just starting out who handled Caro and Hockney, and Grabowski was certainly one of them. He was interesting because he was showing quite avant-garde work, really good quite contemporary work by young sculptors. He had come over from Poland in the 1940s. His son wanted to be an artist and died young, then Grabowski decided to have a gallery and to show artists' work including his son's work. And all this happened after his son died, as far as I know.

Grabowski had earned his money as a pharmacist, he was very successful, and he had a pharmacy in South Kensington. There were two roads that straddled his property, the front of the property was the gallery, a big gallery with three or four rooms in it as far as I remember, and there was a door in the back with an office and another door at the back of the office which actually led into the pharmacy on the other road adjacent to the gallery, which was where you went in to shop for the pharmacy.

I didn't know how successful he was at that time, when he was showing the art of different people like Bridget Riley and John Hoyland. Peter Atkinson, my sculpture teacher from Croydon, had taken me to an exhibition there of work by students from St Martin's when I was still at Croydon, and so when I left St Martin's I took along some photographs of my stuff, including my end of the third year exhibition, and he seemed quite pleased with it. He'd already seen a number of my colleagues so he decided to put on an exhibition of St Martin's students and some other students from another art school, a mixed exhibition of ex-students' work.

I can't remember what I showed the first time, but he liked my work so he decided to show me after that once a year and I think I had three or maybe four exhibitions there. They weren't one-man exhibitions, I remember sharing with a guy called Brian Crouch who was a painter who taught at Kingston School of Art. We got on really well and he actually tried to get me a job at Kingston School of Art but the Head asked me how I was going to teach students when I actually looked younger than his students, because I did look young for my age. I was 21 then and after being at art school from 15 I was quite knowledgeable but he just didn't think that I would have the authority or experience to deal with students.

I'd got enough money to set myself up, I'd got a studio and I was still living in the Victorian house at Parkhill Rise in Croydon. It was just me, by that time, most of my student friends had decided to go to other places but I quite liked still being in Croydon because it was relatively cheap to live at that time. I had a really nice room, a very big room with a bay window, which had a sprung floor. It had been sprung for teaching ballet, so you can tell the size of the room, it was very big. I had a room off that which I used as my studio and drove everybody mad because I was using a jigsaw on aluminium at that time which was incredibly loud. It's always the problem with being a sculptor because you do make a lot of noise at it and most of the time I've lived and worked in residential areas. People can get nasty about it.

I decided I needed to get myself up early in the mornings, so I took a job at a local newsagent and tobacconist, starting at 6 o'clock in the morning. I just sorted out the papers for the paper boys to deliver and it was a couple of hours but it was enough. So at 8 o'clock in the morning I came back with a croissant and coffee and then started work.

I had a friend called de Eskill who was working for Henry Moore, and he set up an interview for me. I remember arriving at Much Hadham for this interview and Henry was very nice and took me all over his house, showed me all his things. He had quite a collection of African sculpture, and all sorts of other people's work. He took me over the garden and into the studios. I think he was most probably working on the sculpture for the UNESCO building in Paris at that time, I'm not sure, but there was a big polystyrene sculpture happening in a sort of prefabricated studio in the garden.

Then he took me to what he called the print room where he did his printing, lithographs or etchings or whatever. In there was a big cabinet with the maquettes in and that was the thing I loved about the visit. The maquettes were really gorgeous but I didn't think much of the later big work, it was being blown up by technicians and I think it's all right to have people working for you, lots of sculptors do, Rodin did it, Michelangelo presumably did it, but you've got to keep an eye on people and you've also got to make a wise decision about how you scale it up. When the UNESCO sculpture was finished and put up outside the UNESCO building in Paris, it is the wrong scale for the building, it's too small. That's the difference between now and the Renaissance, trying to put public sculpture up with buildings that are five or six times the size buildings were in the Renaissance, the sculptures are just dwarfed. It's a good case maybe for making buildings like sculpture in a way rather than just plain blocks, like Frank Gehry's Guggenheim Museum in Bilbao, I do like that and that looks more like a sculpture.

Moore and I got on all right, but I didn't like the way he kept telling me that he came from a working class background. I think he thought I didn't come from the working class, I think he thought I came from some sort of middle class background, because he kept hammering it into me how he'd come from this very working class background. And I thought, well, considering that until I was 14, I had to put up with no electricity in the house, just gas, no television, I don't really like being lectured to just because I came from a southern working class background.

He asked me if I was living on my own, so I said, well, I've got a girlfriend, and he said, are you living together and I said no. He seemed to think that was very funny that I should have a girlfriend. I suppose because I looked so young, he didn't expect it. I'd been going out with this girl for five years so it was quite an emotional tie at the time. I don't think he was that impressed with me and I wasn't too impressed with him. I liked these maquettes, but he was very full of himself. It would have been a good opportunity in some ways, because he was good to his technicians. He owned terraced houses in the village which they could live in. My friend de Eskill was living in one, and I think they were all quite happy there, it was quite a laid-back situation. But anyway nothing came of it and I'm rather pleased I didn't get it I because once you're in that technician job you're stuck in it.

I'd also started working for Anthony Caro. We'd had to move some pieces of his down to a vicarage in Chelsea where he was showing some of his work, that's partly because he was doing very big stuff and I suppose it was better than renting storage for it, so it was in this vicarage garden and then curators and people like that came and he showed them around in quite beautiful surroundings.

I worked with him and we were actually paid by Kasmin. Kasmin and Caro were quite friendly, it wasn't just a business thing. They were both Jewish and Kasmin had started this really nice gallery in Bond Street which again was one of the only avant-garde galleries in London, and he showed Caro. He'd got some pictures by David Hockney, and he actually asked me one day when I was round there talking what I thought of Hockney, did I think that he was any good and I said I quite liked them. David Hockney used to come in to St Martin's to have discussions about art. There was a general mood to get other people involved in St Martin's, as I said before, people like Alexander Trocchi who didn't get paid because he was so heavily on drugs, but he was quite an interesting guy, and Gustav Metzger, the auto-destructive artist, who used to throw acid on his pictures and destroy them. There was one particular time where this happened up on the balcony in the new Hayward Gallery, when it had just opened.

Camden Arts Centre had a look at five or six of my maquettes and they said 'we'll give you a big exhibition'. I borrowed the money to make the full-sized sculptures from my grandmother and then when I phoned them up they said 'oh no we don't want them any more' and there was nothing I could do about it. I had to pay my grandmother back because she didn't have a lot of money and it was quite a lot of money for the time, it was about £200 which actually in the 1960s was a hell of a lot.

I wasn't destitute – because I'd sold those sculptures at Grabowski I was all right for living expenses, but because I was between moving from one of the Victorian houses in Croydon and into the house between Thornton Heath and Norwood I had this awful time when I had nowhere to live, and my grandmother said: 'come and live with us, me and your grandfather'. My grandfather was still working then, and he used to walk to work for 6 o'clock in the morning. They had a spare bedroom, and it was quite nice actually moving back with my grandparents, because these were the same grandparents I'd spent the first four or five years of my life with. There was something much more settled about them than my parents, and I didn't dislike it, it was very strange because I'd lived on my own since I was 15, about eight or nine years by then, but I had to pay all this money back. I didn't have any sex life because my girlfriend couldn't come down so that was a bit of a problem, a restriction, but in another way it was quite nice.

Because they weren't well off, I had to work to pay them back, and I applied to British Railways. They were eager to have me because obviously I'd got references from when I'd worked with them when I was a student, and they put me at Streatham Yard goods station.

Streatham Yard Goods Depot was on the main London to Brighton line, but it was set back, and it was the place where all the goods came in. They had what are called 'roads' which are where the lines come in, lines that are a dead end, and they have lots of trucks on them. They were called roads, because they were roads down the lines with the trucks parked on either side. Each truck would have a code depending on where it was going, so L1 would be

York, L5 would be Halifax or something, I can't remember them all now, but you chalked these codes on each day, and then big articulated lorries came in with all the packages and stuff from the firms. They came up to a platform where there were funny little three-wheeler vans, and you had to unpack the lorries, code the parcels, stack them up in order on trailers behind the three-wheelers and then go down the roads and stack the packages in the appropriate truck according to the code. You couldn't climb in the trucks from the road because they were up high, but you were on this trolley which was the same height as the trucks. Normally when you get into a coach you go from a platform because those wheels are quite big.

Well, it seems easy, but I started work in late summer, so I had all the winter to go through, in the freezing cold. You're out in the open all the time, there was an old railway coach that we could have our sandwiches and breaks in and a funny outside portable-toilet, so it wasn't great. You had battery lamps and they were always leaking, you had to watch the acid with yourself and with the packages especially if it was foodstuff.

In some ways it was horrible, in other ways it was fun. Most of the people that worked there, the white people had had problems, this was the last job they said that you could get, after they'd been dustmen and got sacked from that, this was the last job. But then there were loads of mainly Jamaicans who lived in South-East London. I can't remember all their names, Francis was one, he was always rowing with me, because he didn't think blacks and whites were equal at all. Smithy became quite a good friend, he had two little daughters and he lived in Thornton Heath and used to send his daughters off every Sunday in their fluorescent green and pink dresses to go to the Baptist church, the gospel church. We were very fond of each other because he was my driver on one of these three wheelers and I was on the back delivering the packages. That was okay actually, we didn't get any time off for sleeping or anything and it was a very tough job, but it was okay, Monday to Friday, I didn't have to work Saturday or Sunday.

If you were willing to work Saturday and Sunday you could be a security person and look after the trucks, because people used to come and break into the trucks and steal stuff. A lot of the goods in those days, in the 1960s, were transported by train, all sorts of things, including food - tinned bully beef, baked beans, and other foodstuff, because nearly everything was in tin cans. Some of the people - not me, I never did it - but some of the regulars used to drop a parcel and take a tin out and this was what they used to have for their dinner in the coach at two o'clock, half past two in the morning or something. They used to do it every day, and when you looked down these 'roads' they were littered with torn off labels and empty tin cans. There was one guy who came from a big goods station called Nine Elms, who used to come with brown sticky paper, so he could undo the packages, take something out and then seal them back up again. And then you'd get silly things, like a big sweet company, I think it was Bassetts, every now and again just before Christmas you'd get a big parcel of jelly babies saying 'thank you very much for not stealing any of our goods'!

I decided to work seven nights a week to pay back the money and I was working 12 hours a day from six o'clock in the evening to six o'clock in the morning. You had to watch yourself that you didn't slip on things, because sometimes it was pouring down with rain, you're still outside delivering, you don't stop, the stuff's got to be got rid of before the morning shift because then the new articulated lorries come in.

After about three months of being there they offered me a checker's job, which I took because it was more money but wished I hadn't because you had to go down into the articulated lorries and check all the parcels. You had to look, see where they were going to and then give them a code. It took me ages to memorise all the codes in England, there's something like 50 or 60, so I had to keep coming back, and you couldn't really see because you had this funny battery light which was pretty dim. There was a checker who had been there for years and of course knew when the lorries came in which lorries had the simple things so he could do thousands of parcels in the time I did ten because I had all the rubbish things, like one lawnmower or one piano or something.

There was a really bad accident because in the dark a lawn mower had been tied up with wire to stop it moving. I couldn't really see, and I undid the wire that was joining it, because there were aluminium bars down the articulated lorry, and they'd tied it up, presumably to stop it from moving. So I untied it, but what I didn't realise because I couldn't see very well was that it had a shield over the blades, and that had come off. When the porter came in to remove it he picked it up, the blade turned around, it sliced his thumb and he had to go to hospital and have stitches. He was off for something like 3 months with a sliced thumb. I had to do an accident report and really it was neither of our faults because you couldn't see with these lights, they were so bad, and you were trying to get it done quickly. He didn't blame me, it wasn't a question of blaming, I mean, in some ways, he got a hell of a lot of time off, to be with his kids, but he was a very slow porter and so there were jokes, and also he came from Africa not from Jamaica and so there were the jokes from the Jamaicans, 'oh, that was a clever way of getting rid of him, because he was so slow', the sort of male sense of humour, but no real bitterness, I have to say there was no bitterness.

I used to argue with some of the whites, because there was still a lot of racism then and they used to say awful things and I used to have a go at them. By and large I got on with the Jamaicans better than anyone else, there was one guy who was working there at nights and trying to go to university.

There was another incident once when I was doing security on a Sunday night when one of the porters, there was always supposed to be two, and he said 'I'm just going to go out and get a hamburger' or something, so I said 'don't be long because I'm here on my own'. We used to sit in the coach where we had our tea, and at regular times we had to patrol the roads with all the trucks on, you're talking about a hundred trucks or more, I don't know how many, but rows and rows of them. Some of the roads as you got further away from the centre where the platform was there was hardly any light so you were in the dark. He went and of course he was gone an hour and suddenly I heard all this banging, so I thought 'I'd better go and see what it is'. I did have a big searchlight thing, like a big torch, and in the coach there was a red telephone to call the railway police. I'd got out of the coach because I wasn't quite sure where the banging was coming from and I walked half way down one of these rows and then realised that somebody was breaking in to the end coach. So I phoned up the railway police. The other guy, who'd just cleared off, gone to a late night party or something, came back just before the railway police arrived and he was sitting in there with his tin of condensed milk making himself a cup of tea while I went out and sorted it with the police.

There were about ten policemen, with four Alsatian dogs. I started going down this row of trucks showing them where it was and I got all the way down to the end and there was still some commotion going on, they hadn't gone, and I turned round and the police were miles behind me and I thought 'what's their game?' So I turned back and I said 'you're the police, you deal with it!' and I went off. They never caught them, but it made me laugh because I was so far ahead of the police, it was their job to be ahead of me.

And then I had another scare. It was pouring hard with rain and I got the train from Croydon to Streatham Yard and got off the train. When you got off the train you had to walk across the lines, and on the London to Brighton line there was a third line, not overhead electricity, a third line. It was pouring down with rain and I remember crossing and it was just like somebody had given me a rabbit punch on the back of my neck. It was just like somebody whacking me but when I looked behind there was nobody behind me at all. When I got into the coach where we were just going to start work, I said to them, 'I just had a weird experience, it was like somebody giving me a rabbit punch' and this old boy who was sitting there said 'you know what you did, you just skimmed the live rail as you went over it. If you'd stuck to it you wouldn't be alive now, you'd be dead'. So it was pretty dangerous stuff, they didn't have the same concerns for health and safety at that time.

There were accidents on the railways. I remember coming home from Brighton once and somebody committed suicide, and that's major, when somebody does that, because the driver saw the person and slammed on the brakes. Because they're metal wheels on metal rails it wears the wheel down, it actually takes the metal off the wheels, because you've jammed on the brakes. It wears it flat, instead of it being circular it makes a flat bit on the wheel and then we had to limp into the station because as the wheel went round it went 'clunk, clunk, clunk'. We couldn't get any further than the next station, we all had to get out and get the next train, and the poor driver got carted off, because witnessing something like that is terrible. It's heavy work. I was talking to an engine driver while he was driving electric coaches, and he said he'd worked on the underground and he didn't like that at all because people are always committing suicide on the underground, he said 'they're always throwing themselves in front of the trains'.

It took me the best part of three quarters of a year to pay my grandparents off. I was still managing to make art in that time, even though I only had a little bedroom, I just had a single bed in there and I was painting four foot canvases and making maquettes like mad. And in a way it was good that I was living with my grandparents because I didn't have to do anything, my granny used to cook for me, and make sandwiches for me for the night, so she really did look after me like a mum, all I had to do was work 12 hours a day. I generally used to get home about seven and then I used to sleep to about two, and then I had two or three hours before I had to think about getting back to work again, so I did have a couple of hours and I used to read stuff, mostly novels. I wasn't around when the television was on, there was no afternoon television in those days. I did quite a few paintings there, I made some maquettes, but life had changed drastically, and it was only a few years previously that I was at St Martin's and having exhibitions, so I wasn't too pleased.

Chapter 5 - Grange Road 1967-70

I managed to pay off my grandparents so I didn't have to work for British Railways any more, but I wasn't in a great place in my life. I'd worked briefly for Caro, but the pay wasn't very good. I'd had the interview with Henry Moore but nothing came from that. I went to see if I could become a teacher and they said I would have to do teacher training and I thought what do I want to do that for? I'd just done six years of art school but they said, 'well you've got to learn how to teach'. I didn't want to go back to college where most of the time I couldn't make art, I just felt a couple of years just solid writing wasn't in me.

A college friend suggested that I work for the Inner London Education Authority, doing Play Centre, which was an activity that happened after school finished, at 4 o'clock, and basically you were child-minding until the parents came and picked the children up. It was a five day a week thing from 4 o'clock till about 6 or 6.30. It was good because I could teach the kids drawing or painting, or I could play football with the boys or some other activity. Generally the person who was in charge of it decided what they wanted you to do with the children and of course it brought in a bit more money during the Christmas and Easter and the six weeks summer vacation when we would work full time.

I didn't just work in one school, I worked all over the place, sometimes on the Isle of Dogs, sometimes in Peckham, sometimes Dulwich and other places. That was quite interesting, to see different children, but I was still looking for a job where I could earn enough money to make my sculpture.

A rather gruesome thing happened when I was working for the Play Centre that harked back to my days working on the railways. There was a boy of about seven who had watched a Western film about a man listening for a train by putting his ear to the railway line because of the vibrations. This young boy wanted to try it out, and by mistake he'd put his ear to the live line. Luckily his friend had the sense to pull him off. The friend got first degree burns to his hand and the little boy got his eye burnt out and his legs welded together. He survived though, they stitched him up, they separated his legs. He had a patch over one eye, but he was lucky to survive.

I'd had to move out of the Victorian house because Wates wanted it so they could demolish it and build some more of their little cardboard box houses, so I'd had to find new accommodation. I met up with an old friend who had also studied sculpture at Croydon, Gerald McCarthy, and we found a flat to share between Thornton Heath and Upper Norwood, overlooking Grange Park. It was quite a nice flat, but it was on the first floor, and the problem for me was it didn't have anywhere for me to work. It was just the two rooms, Gerry lived in one and I lived in the other, then a communal kitchen that he and I used and a completely communal bathroom that was used by all three floors. So there was nowhere for me to work at all.

I did a lot of drawing while I lived there, I used to go down into the park to draw. Also Gerry was interested in photography, and I was quite interested in using photography and always have been. I'd done some with my friend John Groves, who was a graphics student at Croydon when we lived in the first Victorian house, and some more when I was at St Martin's. Gerry and I decided to turn the kitchen into a dark room, so we were actually eating our food in the dark most of the time, with all these photographic chemicals around. But I still needed a studio to make sculpture.

At the first showing of my work at Grabowski after I left St Martin's I met up again with a fellow student I'd known and been friendly with at St

Martin's, a really nice woman called Jane Armstrong. She was older than me, a part-time mature student with three children, and she and her husband David lived in West Dulwich. When she heard I'd got nowhere to do my metalwork, she said: 'Well, why don't you come and work in our garage, it's a big double garage and there's plenty of room there'. She said 'I've got oxy-acetylene equipment for welding, you can share that'.

It was about a 25 minute walk from the flat through Gypsy Hill down Alleyn Road into Dulwich. It was quite a nice walk, and I used to go over there every day to make my sculpture, and I became quite friendly with them. A couple of times I babysat for them. I never paid them for the use of the studio and they didn't want anything, they were quite happy having me there.

I also became friendly with Jane's mother, Mollie Trevelyan, who lived in Cambridge. She was from the Winchester-Bennet family of New England, and had married one of the Trevelyans, so there was a lot of money there. They had a very big beautiful house at Gazeley in Cambridge, and she had quite a lot of children, I can't remember all of them, but as I said her daughter Jane was at St Martin's with me and we became friends. I did a huge piece of sculpture, which Grabowski didn't sell, and they took it, because they had this huge, beautiful garden. I came up to visit her, and that was the first time I'd been to Cambridge. I had about four pieces there at one time and I was very grateful to them, they were good people, the Trevelyans and Jane and David Armstrong, they were good friends to me and they bought some of my work.

At the Play Centre where I was working there was a woman, Mrs Cady, who also worked full-time at a private school, Hill House Prep School. I didn't quite understand at the time why she had to come and do the Play Centre as well, why what she earned in the school wasn't enough, but I found out she needed the money to pay for private health care for her daughter, who was dying of cancer. She told me she'd keep an eye out if any vacancies came up at the school. One day when I saw her at work she said that the teacher who was teaching art had left and the Headmaster was looking for somebody to take over. She said 'I've already talked to him about you and if you arrive on such and such a date and time he'll interview you'.

I went there and met the Headmaster, Colonel Townend, and he took a liking to me, I don't know why because I didn't know really whether I wanted to teach in a private school at that time, but I was short of the money and he was the only person who was willing to give me a job. I didn't work full days at first, I worked from about 9 till 2 in the afternoon, but that changed, and in the end I was doing four full days and then having one day off. He was okay, but I thought his politics were a bit doubtful, he was always singing the praise of the 1936 Olympics so I didn't know quite what he thought of Hitler, I think he might have thought at the time that Hitler was quite a good man. There were things that we didn't agree about, but I was there for about four or five years and he was very good to me. I wasn't earning great money but I was probably earning what teachers earned in the state school system at that time, and of course it was good for me because I was picking up information about teaching which I would have had to do teacher's training for, and I wasn't working the hours I would have had to do in the state system.

Gerry eventually moved out of the flat we were sharing, but I managed, with the money I earned from teaching, to take it over myself and stay there on my own. I mentioned before that I have a great interest in plants since I was first at art school in Croydon, and when I was in the flat I had some begonias, which were the first real plants that I'd ever kept. They were in the main room, in a hanging basket in front of a long elongated window with three panels of leaded lights. It was my room, I used to sleep in it but it was mainly my studio and I just had a bed in the corner. The window overlooked the park keeper's house in Grange Park where I used to go and draw.

I walked up Grange Road past the park and down Gypsy Hill to the studio in West Dulwich every day and walked back which was maybe a mile or two miles each way. There was an old man who lived around there, I never met him, but he used to let his dog out every day in the park and the dog would stay in the park. I didn't know anything about this but the dog took a fancy to me because I was always sitting in the park drawing. I did a lot of drawings of the park, one of the things as well as doing my sculpture was to draw all the pathways going through the park with the trees. I felt I needed to as I'd got out of the habit of doing observational drawing, because all the way through St Martin's I hadn't done that much drawing. The only drawing I'd done was very vague ideas for sculpture in a very abstract manner, so I hadn't been drawing people. At Croydon for three years I spent three days a week almost all drawing and I hadn't done much drawing since, so I thought 'well, I've got to get back into it' and I started doing these conté drawings,

46

very dark, quite morbid in a way I think now, looking back at them. I would sit in the park for hours, if I wanted a break from the sculpture, and there was always this dog who took a liking to me. He just used to sit there beside me and I used to stroke him and I used to see him every time I went in the park. The park keeper came up to me one day and he said 'did you know that dog waits for you?' and that's when he told me that he was the dog of an old man who couldn't get out so he used to let the dog out.

The dog was a dachshund, very close to the ground with short little legs and great big floppy ears, and his name was Ben. Ben and I got on really well. It was the only time I ever wanted a dog, in fact I often think if I had a dog it would either be a collie, because I like collies too, or a dachshund. A funny little dog it was, but that's what I used to do.

I started observational drawings and they were very dark, looking back at them, and quite morbid in a funny sort of way. There was one pencil drawing which I sold, which was a drawing of the trees and the path but also the sunlight coming through the trees, so it's dappled with shadows and things. I was interested in space, the space of the trees apart but also the light between.

In the meantime I had met up with an old friend of mine, Paul Lansom. He'd stayed on at Croydon when I went to St Martin's, because you could stay at Croydon and do painting, but if you wanted to go on to do sculpture there was only the equivalent to a foundation or first year of a BA. We met up and used to see each other socially now and again and take trips off to the Tate Britain, well the Tate Gallery it was then, there was only the one, and the new Hayward Gallery had just opened or was just about to open, and in the evenings we used to gad around London.

We both got interested in Zen Buddhism, partly through the paintings of Mark Tobey, who was an American abstract expressionist who'd studied with a Zen Master. I used to go to a little bookshop in South Kensington on my way home from work in Knightsbridge, and I bought a book on oriental art. There's a lot of people like Basho who was a Zen master who did paintings and sculptures, quite simple things. If they had been exhibited without a name you might have thought they were abstract expressionist paintings or something from the 1960/70s, but in fact they were these Zen masters. I'm not sure what period it would have been. Buddhism came from India to China, and then you get the stories, Pigsy, Sandy and Tripitaki, from the classic Monkey stories by Wu Ch'engen and then Buddhism went to Japan, so I was particularly interested in Zen and the Zen paintings like Mu Chi's *Six Persimmons* in the 13th century and Basho in the 17th century.

So because there was always that influence on the American School, very Japanese, very simple, we got interested in Buddhism, Mahayana and Hinayana it means large vehicle and small vehicle. Through that we got quite interested in Zen and we used to take ourselves off to the Buddhist Society, which was then run by Christmas Humphreys, the judge. The Buddhist Society was all right, but it wasn't like a practising Buddhism that you get a lot of places now. We're talking about early days, the Beatles had just gone off to India a couple of years before, and stuff like that, so it was early days for my generation to be influenced by Buddhist spirituality and different religious beliefs. I think in mine and Paul's case it was partly that we were just intrigued by a different outlook on life rather than Christianity, which fitted in somehow to the artistic process. I don't know if we talked about it a lot. One of the big things we used to talk about a lot at St Martin's was objectivity and subjectivity and intuition, when do you know when something is finished, things like that. So already there was the core of thinking about a process in art which has if you like a parallel running with Zen.

Then we started to go to the Poetry Society, which was a very strange little place. It always killed us because it was run by little old ladies making cups of tea and biscuits, but some of the poets they had there were forceful characters and used rather strong language. But these little old ladies didn't seem to mind at all.

One night we were in a pub having a beer before going back on the train, and a big black man started talking to us about life, and we started talking about Buddhism and he said 'well come back to my place, you don't have to catch the train you can catch it in the morning and we can talk all night'. Well, he was quite genuine, so we went back with him, it was a really nice place but he was a Scientologist or something and he was trying to sell us this Scientology when we got back to his place. We just found it hilarious.

That's how we used to spend a lot of Saturday evenings. We didn't have much money, sometimes we'd just go to the pub and have a pint of beer and sit there and argue about Zen Buddhism. We used to go off to Bromley and places like that in the car, sometimes we used to go off and have a pint of beer and come back. It was a very simple life, and most of the time we argued about either painting or sculpture or something, and that friendship went on right until into my first marriage.

One day a friend of mine from Croydon School of Art arrived at my flat in Grange Road and said 'I'm giving up the Perspex business'. His name was Peter Holland, he's dead now, he trained as a painter at Croydon but I rather lost track of him going to St Martin's. After Croydon he got himself a load of machinery and found out how to use Perspex acrylic, and he started making jewellery for places like Carnaby Street, it was that time in the 1960s when Carnaby Street was big. So he put together all this machinery for shaping the acrylic sheets, sanding discs and the polishers and the things that I've still got and am using now, 40 years later.

He was the sort of person that when it was successful he gave it up. He obviously wasn't doing it for the money, he should have been a painter really but he never had the confidence, we talked about it years afterwards. He turned up on my doorstep that day and said 'I'm going to throw all this stuff away unless you take it'.

I had a Volkswagen Caravette at the time, so of course, I went down there and collected all the tools and equipment, and the only place I could put it all was in my kitchen. This was the same kitchen that had doubled up as a darkroom, now it doubled up as a workshop, and one half of the kitchen was covered with see-through plastic which was taped up to the wall, the floor and the ceiling, and with holes where I could put my hands and use the machines. There was no dust extraction so I had to contain the dust somehow, so I had to put my hands through these holes that I'd cut in the plastic and that retained a lot of the dust. Of course I got complaints from the neighbours downstairs because of the rumble of the machines and the noise. I was always getting complaints.

But that was where I did my first acrylic pieces. I did the small ones, 20-30 cms high, and somebody came round once and suggested that, because they were small, I should try Editions Alecto. Editions Alecto did reproductions, mainly prints but they were into doing reproductions of sculpture too, I think they might have done some reproductions of Eduardo Poalozzi, I'm not sure. I went off to see them and showed them the slides and they were very interested. They said 'bring us six or seven and we'll reproduce them'.

I took seven and didn't hear any more from them, a couple of months went by, the usual thing, so I thought 'well I'll give them a ring'. They had given me a piece of paper saying that they'd accepted the seven and I had that, signed by them and stamped and everything, saying that they'd got seven of my pieces of sculpture. I phoned them up and they said 'We haven't seen any of your sculptures' so I went all the way into London to see them and they said: 'we're sorry but we thought you'd taken them away'. I showed them the piece of paper so they couldn't deny that they'd had them and they said: 'we thought you'd come to collect them' and I said 'no, if I had I would have signed something to say I'd taken them, wouldn't I?' They started being a bit fishy then, they didn't want to know. So I went round to this rather swish police station in Savile Row. Of course they weren't very helpful they just took one look at the slides of my sculptures and said 'is this sculpture?'

In the course of going over to West Dulwich and working in the studio, I used to have a chat and a cup of tea with Jane, just like I am with you, so I told her about what had happened, and she rang her family solicitor straightaway, and he agreed to see me. His name was Mr Kimberley, I can't remember his first name.

He had an office in the Temple and of course I then had to find this place and it was difficult because there are so many of them in there. I was absolutely overawed because I didn't even know it existed. When I found him he was really nice, a very intelligent man, he was most probably in his 40s then. Of course I was young and he said 'oh, are you going to be another Henry Moore?' and he was really interested. He said 'don't worry, you've got the letter, there's no way they can wangle out of this' he said 'I'm going to write a letter and they'll come up with the money as soon as they get it'. I thought 'he's got a hope', but a week later he wrote to me saying 'I've got your money, a cheque' and that was that. I don't know what he said in the letter, but he obviously stated the facts and he said to me 'you did well by getting something signed, always in the future make sure you get something from them in writing'.

The next thing that happened later on, when I needed to use his services again, was when I had an exhibition at Kodak House and they took seven small sculptures off me, and they also showed about eight really big sculptures. Well, the eight big sculptures were fine, the seven small ones disappeared, just like Editions Alecto, and I couldn't believe it. It was a funny situation at Kodak House because it was all under lock and key, they were all kept in glass cabinets, and the guy admitted that they must have been taken internally. The Editions Alecto people, they didn't admit that they'd been taken internally because they'd actually had builders in so they could have been taken by the builders, they just didn't look to see. At Kodak House the guy who organised the exhibition was very nice, and he said it had happened one Saturday night when they had a social gathering. He knew when it happened but of course he didn't know who'd taken them, but he put a thing in the firm's paper saying how awful it was. I just went off to Mr Kimberley again and I got paid again, I don't know what he put in these letters.

And I didn't get charged by him, presumably the Trevelyan family picked it up which was really nice of them.

Chapter 6 - New York and After 1970-72

After about four years of teaching at Hill House, I was pretty fed up with teaching private children. They were good kids and I was very fond of them, it wasn't their fault they were being sent to private school, and there were some really very talented boys.

One of the English teachers there had friends in New York and he suggested, 'why don't we go off to New York and see if there's work there?' I'd written to David Smith the sculptor when I'd left college to try and become his technician, but unfortunately, although he probably did get my letter, David Smith had died coming home from a party about the same time, he hit a tree in his truck and he died, so that ruled that out. But I was quite interested to see the David Smith estate, which was in Vermont.

My friend Jane Armstrong also knew people in New York, she knew a Jewish woman in Dulwich whose sister and brother in law, Fran and Steve, lived in New York, and I went to stay with them. Steve was a lawyer, I'm not quite sure what Fran did, but she was just expecting their first baby at the time. They lived in Brooklyn and I really enjoyed New York, the Metropolitan, the Guggenheim, the Witney, it was great.

I had an interview at a place called Marion which was a secondary kind of College which was looking for an art teacher. So I left Fran and Steve and went on my journeys up the east coast and called in there and was interviewed by this very nice man. I didn't know whether to stay there or not at the time. I thought, well, is this going to be interesting? I was unsure because I thought I might end up back in the same situation I was in at the school in Knightsbridge.

I went to Boston, to Harvard and Massachusetts Institute of Technology, where they were doing some interesting experiments with vibrating sound on plates, which gave the same pattern if the tuning of the vibration was the same but changed with different tuning. That's when I got to know about people like Buckminster-Fuller, the engineer. They were very friendly and showed me around, and I went places like the Fogg Art Museum.

But as life would have it, just before I left for America my grandmother had died, the one who had been so pivotal in my upbringing. I didn't react at the time but I was conscious of the loss and when I came back from America and was deciding whether to take the job or not I found myself back in the flat on my own. I was extremely depressed, in part because I was missing my grandmother, and I began to get really quite upset about things, not emotionally but I was not right.

That's when I started to change because when I came back I used to go and see my grandfather. He would be eating alone and that's how *Table for One* came about, subconsciously, I didn't know what I was doing I just started to make this sculpture. When I'd made it I realised, I knew there was something about it, it was like a table but it didn't have a top. I was reading Buckminster-Fuller at the time, he was the designer of the geodesic dome. From my visits to the Massachusetts Institute of Technology when I was in Boston, I was quite into ergonomics and I understood about ergonomics, how chairs are just the right size for us and so on. I started thinking about why I felt so secure with my grandparents, because they had these big old armchairs, and of course as a child they seem massive to you. It's a different sort of ergonomics, because you feel quite contained within this armchair, so that was sort of psychological too. Then I started thinking about this sculpture in terms of ergonomics. It had got space underneath it where you could put your legs, but of course it wasn't a table, and I didn't think at the time that people would understand what it was about, so I wrote a poem that was supposed to be exhibited with the sculpture.

Table for One was about my grandfather eating alone. I suddenly realised that a table is either round or has four sides, it's a social thing, it's not just a functional thing, it's a psychological thing, it's an emotional thing. Tables have multiple functions, and as I wrote in the poem, people even make love on tables. I remember turning a whole table upside down and pretending it was a boat when I was a kid, like the Ship of Fools, the *Raft of the Medusa*. So tables have all sorts of different connotations.

I didn't realise at the time, but it really did upset me to see him just eating alone. He was in a bad state when my grandmother died, he wanted to die, basically, he was suffering from a broken heart, and it took him two years to wear himself down. I suppose that's understandable, it's a different generation, they had been together virtually all their adult life. He was 80 something when he died, it's a long time to be together if you come together when you're 15 as she was, and I think he was only about a year or two older than she was. It's an awful long time, to be with somebody over 60 years, and he just couldn't take it. She was his security I suppose.

I was going there every week to see him, every Tuesday, and we discussed living together, but there was no way I could have him in my place and he had a small flat so I couldn't have taken all my work there. In the end he went to live with my parents, but he didn't last long there because he was already on the decline.

Table for One was exhibited at various places, I'm not sure whether it was exhibited at the Trade Union Congress with *Famine* and *Shelter*, but I think I exhibited it at Kodak House and the Digswell Art Trust. It was quite a departure because it was very simple. It was made up of aluminium and Perspex and it was a very simple construction but it had a lot of psychological meaning to it, and that's when it got me thinking about making sculpture for other uses rather than just for itself, for actually saying something about the human condition or society. Although that sounds new it wasn't because when I was at St Martin's I had actually sketched out some ideas for *Famine* but I never had the apparatus, I didn't know how to do it. The first famine I became conscious of was when I was at St Martin's, which I think was Biafra, and I knew I wanted to do something. In fact one of the problems I always had with being an abstract artist was that I felt I did have to communicate other things. Now I'm much more resigned to it, because after all Bach's Brandenburg Concertos are just Bach's Brandenburg Concertos, they haven't got any other meaning, they are exercises in abstract music, if you like. But at the time, partly most probably because of this other crisis, my mental crisis, which was about dislocation I suppose, I started thinking of ways in which I could pull things together.

Table for One was very abstract, in fact they all were except for *Famine*. *Famine* was the only one you could call figurative. *Shelter* was quite abstract too, and I made a number of very different sculptures. The one called *In Memory* is like a gravestone in Perspex and aluminium which you can see through, and I put it on the grass so you could see the grass through it. That was to do with my grandfather, and so I made two sculptures really emanating from his death, *In Memory* and *Table for One*.

So my grandparents' death really did affect my sculpture, it affected me and it affected my sculpture, and I suppose it was the biggest contribution to me having therapy. My grandfather died before I had therapy, and that was a big contribution.

Ergonomics and psychology played quite an important part in how I was behaving at that time, and *Table for One* was actually made just before my first wife came to live with me at the flat with her daughter, so before we left for St Ives I'd already made *Table for One*. The pieces I was making were quite minimal constructions with aluminium holding them together. I made *In Memory* and then when I was at St Ives I made *Sport* and later I made *Window* and *Chair*. *Chair* was about sitting down, so that was more to do with ergonomics.

In the first year at St Martin's Caro used to give us projects to do. I really liked these projects, and I think my first piece of metal sculpture was done for a project. We were sent to the science museum to make something, and the first piece there was *Inside Out*, which has always stayed with me. Some of these projects are to do with history of sculpture. *Inside Out* was a Bauhaus project as far as I know, so they weren't necessarily what Caro had thought up, they were current in sculpture from the modernist period, they were to do with the Russian Constructivists, the Bauhaus and so on. One of the projects we were given was 'what's the feeling of sitting down?', so I did a bent piece of wood with a plaster shape in it and it sort of echoed the way that your bottom is when you sit down.

I thought about that again when I was doing *Table for One*, and when I did *Chair*. *Chair* was about a construction that took the same space as a chair but it didn't have any seat. It was about the way in which when you go to sit down, you don't put your hands on the seat and then lower yourself down, unless there's something wrong with you, you just take a chance. And it's about that letting go, which fitted in with the letting go that I was reading about in Zen Buddhism.

When I was with Paul I managed to get hold of an old copy of Suzuki's *Zen in the Art of Archery*, and that was one of the big influences for me in Zen. The whole idea with *Zen in the Art of Archery* is you can aim a bow and arrow at the target but there are two things really I suppose that came out of that. I don't want to go into great detail about it but one is that you get your whole body ready for that, the muscles and everything, not just the arm muscles. The other thing is the letting go of the arrow, because it is a Zen discipline, the letting go of the arrow. It's very difficult to describe, it was very difficult for me to get it at first when it was written down in the book, because you're thinking well what do they mean, because the whole thing is that the target is you and it's about you being able to let go of things.

All that influenced this development of how I made *Table for One* and those other sculptures about the human condition. They were to do with the process of making art, but also saying something about the human condition and with *Table for One* and *Chair* they were about ergonomics, so as I was saying, *Chair* was to do with that sensation you have of letting go and trusting the chair is there. Of course there's that awful thing when you're at school when somebody whips the chair away so that's what I was up to with the chair business. Those were the sort of ideas that were surrounding me when I was in Grange Road and then also later when I was at St Ives.

The time after I came back from America, after the death of first my grandmother and then my grandfather, was very difficult for me, and the very dark conté drawings that I was doing in the park outside the flat were in a way a precursor to this. Now I realise that subconsciously they were reflecting this very morbid dark side of my personality which was quite suicidal. I suppose

I'd always thought of suicide and always thought it was the norm to think about it. I'd never discussed that even with Paul and the first people I started to discuss it with were Jane and David Armstrong and Graham Davis, a psychoanalyst, who rented the top floor flat with his family. His wife Lizzie was a poet who I got along with very well and I had a lot of correspondence with her because she used to read my poetry and I used to comment on hers. It was rather a strange situation because I think she and Graham had started to part at that point. I met her family, and I got to know her two younger brothers, not so much Benjamin, the younger one, although he was really nice, because he was too young, but the other one, Paul, I got to know well and in fact put him up for some time at my flat because he had nowhere to live, and he was going to Croydon School of Art as a student. So it was quite a strong connection between me and Lizzie.

I started getting all sorts of pains in my stomach, and I got a terrible pain in my groin and went along to the doctor and at first they couldn't find anything. I talked to Graham and he said 'I think you need help because you're really not well', he said, ' 'I think most of the pains you're getting are psychosomatic'. He got me certified and because of that I was able to get into the Tavistock Institute on the National Health. That's how I got my therapy, which looking back was a real godsend to me, because I didn't really realise how badly I was suffering. I was most probably manic-depressive, I suppose, that was mentioned to me a couple of times.

I started seeing a psychiatrist called Dr Goldblatt. He was a very laid back man to say the least, he didn't say very much I didn't know how the procedure worked, it took me some time to work out the procedure there, just letting me talk.

But what established itself in the end was there were three things I needed to look at. One was the relationship between me and my grandmother and my relationship with my mother because they were very very different. The other thing was the death of my grandmother because I really hadn't come to terms with that, and also the death of Peter, the friend I had seen die on his bicycle when I was thirteen. That was a big trauma for me at the time, seeing Peter die, and nobody asked me if I'd seen, and so I didn't tell a soul that I'd seen it until I was an adult. I said to Dr Goldblatt it was quite a big shock for a young boy, to be confronted by death like that, because if you can imagine it's like a child believing in Santa Claus and then suddenly waking up to find Dad and Mum putting the stuff in the sock.

Life was never the same for me after Peter died because I knew that our existence was very fragile, and the doctor said that because I had that knowledge so young, I hadn't really come to terms with it, because I'd never really grieved about anybody and he said that indicated the fact that I'd wanted to when I was at school. As soon as we got into assembly I wanted to go to the toilet, every morning I'd go to the toilet and then as soon as I sat down in assembly I'd want to go again.

He said, didn't you tell anybody about it? And one of the problems I had was that I just didn't communicate with people, and he thought that was to do with my mother because she never really took notice of me, it was all about her, so it was useless me trying to communicate anything to her. And then by the time Peter had died I wasn't living with my grandmother, I stopped living with my grandmother when I was four or five so that was more distant, so I just never told anybody.

Goldblatt worked on me and got me to work on myself and then I met my first wife. It was a bit foolish of me really because when you fall in love you think the world is absolutely wonderful and it wasn't because I was still having the pain.

In the meantime when I was having analysis, suddenly my right testicle decided to take off and become about eight times bigger than it should have been. It was so big I couldn't walk around so they had me in hospital. They thought it was cancer of the testicle, they actually told me they might have to take the testicle away, or both the testicles, and so at the age of 29 I was lying in there thinking, oh my God, if I go down, in a couple of hours I might come back and that's my sex life gone, so that was traumatic too. And of course there were no scans in those days. When I woke up, I'll never forget it, I felt down there as soon as I woke up, I had both of them, but the right one was like an ice cube, and because the testicles have to keep warm to manufacture the sperm. I freaked out because it was completely cold. The Sister came over, she was very good to me, and she said 'don't worry, you've just been operated on, the doctor will be in to tell you what they're going to do and what they've done' and she said, 'just keep calm and wait for the doctor, the doctor has promised that he'll be in as soon as you're awake'.

Well, he did come in, while the Sister was there, and he said 'we've taken a bit of your testicle, we've made you sterile on that side for a start'. They couldn't actually see any abnormal growth, they took some of it out and put it back in again, and that's why it was cold, and he said it would take a couple weeks for the analysis to come back to see whether I was going to be okay. He said 'hopefully it's not going to be cancerous, it didn't look cancerous. The size of it is being caused by something else we're not sure what it is, we've yet to find out what the cause of it is', and in fact they never really found what had caused it.

I had a girlfriend at the time, we were all right, we weren't living together and we didn't have much in common, I don't really know why I got involved with her, but anyway one day I was walking to hers for dinner, and I bumped into Maxie, who was to become my first wife.

Maxie was a student at Croydon with me and she'd always fancied me, and we'd had a little affair which lasted about two weeks before I'd decided to break it off. But when I met her again she said she was living with her husband, it wasn't going well, she'd got her 18-month-old daughter Laura with her and she said she'd come round and see me. In the end we decided to live together, and that was problematic because she actually came to see me in hospital when my other girlfriend was there too, and my mother. It ended up with a huge shouting match not actually in the ward, in the waiting room, and this Irish Sister, the one that was good to me, came in and said 'I've just asked your mother to leave and never to come back! Do you mind?' I was quite pleased that somebody could stand up to my mother.

Anyway, Maxie brought me in these beautiful alstroemerias, lilies, they were orange streaked with dark blue, absolutely beautiful, I haven't seen alstroemerias like them since. We started living together with her daughter Laura and of course that was where I became involved with a marriage bust-up. I hadn't been married before but there was Laura's father to consider, Mike. He was a very nice man and he used to see Laura at least once a week on a Sunday. It wasn't nasty, but looking back the marriage wasn't quite as on the rocks as she'd made it out to be, I don't think, she just wanted a change. And Mike was really upset about it, I remember him crying on me once, and that didn't go down very well at all, because I was having my doubts by then.

But we did stay together and she said she thought it was best if I stopped seeing the analyst now, she'd sort me out. That was rather premature and he told me that, and he said 'Well I think you've got enough to go on, and you shouldn't really rely on other people, you've got to do it yourself' and I thought well, I think I've got enough to go on with, and looking back I don't regret it. I think it might have been good for me to do another year, but I do think that what he told me at the time I was still thinking about it in five years time. He really did impress me with what he said, and it changed my mind, my life, because before I went to Goldblatt I was definitely a manic depressive, when I used to get depressed I used to sit and think about suicide virtually every day. I didn't think there was anything wrong with me until I got really ill, but then I'd lived with that all my life, I'd lived with the idea of suicide as being an option. Overnight in a sense he'd alleviated all that, and I felt much better with myself. I still had a lot of work to do on myself, like everybody, confidence, all these things that everybody has to work on, but he'd taught me to think about the times when I went down that I would also go back up again, and that it wasn't so bleak as it seemed. So he made me feel much more objective about my old self and see myself more clearly.

There was one thing that they were quite interested in with me at the Tavistock, and that was because I used to have these out-of-body sessions. They didn't know what caused them, this was fresh ground then. And I got quite interested in all sorts of things because of going there, for instance I got interested in dreams and rapid eye movements, REMs, because we used to work a lot on my dreams, and through Goldblatt I learned to interpret them, I'm quite good at interpreting dreams, not great but I'm beginning to understand links .

At that time the Tavistock was being run by Laing, so I got interested in Lang and started reading him and through Laing I got interested in Jung, who I really did like, the anima and the animus, the male and the female in you, so I was learning a lot about myself at the same time and trying to put that to some sort of use, but also there were these outside body sensations. I'd had the first one when I was at St Martin's, I was standing talking to my then girlfriend Wendy and a technician and then suddenly it was like I was looking down on me and the technician and the girlfriend and you know when you hear your voice on the tape recorder for the first time, well it was that same sort of shock because I'd never seen the back of my head or anything, and I could see the back of me standing there talking and at the same time I felt ill inside, felt this really deep. It's really difficult to describe it. I remember trying to describe it to Dr Goldblatt at the time and he thought that that feeling itself was similar to the feeling you get when you are manic depressive, it's that awful deep down, weighed down thing, so the two things were hand in hand somehow, they were linked. I got interested in these things because by the time I went to see Dr Goldblatt I'd had quite a lot of them, I'd had three or four when I was teaching. It was discussed whether they were a form of epilepsy, not an epileptic fit but a form of epilepsy because I didn't know up until then that one person in four suffers from some form of epilepsy but that doesn't mean to say that they have fits. That was put forward as one of the reasons why I was having them and they carried on and I got quite interested in them because I tried to stay outside of my body and the more I tried to stay outside the more I got this terrible feeling of being ill, so that would get me back inside again, sooner or later.

I wasn't quite sure what caused them, I was quite a heavy smoker, so whether it was lack of oxygen or whatever I don't know, but I haven't had so many recently since I've been older, I think I've had two or three in the last five years. I still get them, and maybe they are brought on by some sort of stress. At the same time, when I started to go with my first wife I started to have migraines. I didn't know that they were migraines at the time, because I didn't get a headache, but they were impairment of the vision, and I think that was caused by stress, because I was quite stressed at the time, but after I stopped seeing Dr Goldblatt, I think he'd impressed me enough and I'd started already to get an interest in thinking about psychology and how it affected me and also how it affected my art, because that came up when I was in the Tavistock, maybe I wasn't doing art, maybe art was some sort of release mechanism or I was using it in some way.

So I was beginning then to think about maybe using my art, that was early days then, but already when you think that I made *Table For One* by 1974, because all the time I was on therapy I was actually visiting my grandfather once a week and seeing him incredibly depressed. The worst thing that I experienced with him was to see him sitting alone at the table eating his dinner because suddenly I realised that tables are not designed for one person, they're designed for sitting around, they're designed for people sitting around having some sort of social activity as well as just eating from. So I'd begun to get quite interested in physical ergonomics, the way we sit at a table, but also I was interested in if you like the mental, the psychological work of ergonomics in how we conduct ourselves when we are faced with a situation where you've been living with somebody and then they're no longer there. So that nucleus of being at the Tavistock led, I think, to quite an important change in my outlook as far as art was concerned.

It was a dreadful time in my life but there wasn't anybody at that time I could really talk to. My mother had no idea what I was suffering, I could have lost both testicles, and all she was interested in was having this row with my future wife. That was awful, I mean, it was really strange, I wasn't a very talkative person, I used to keep it all inside. That was at the same time as I was seeing him, because they weren't quite sure whether it was all psychological, because, the pains wouldn't go away, so they started doing tests on me and the problem with cancer in those days there were no scans. They couldn't x-ray me because they would have sterilised me, you can't x-ray the testicles, you'd actually kill off the sperm. Later on, when I had another operation, they said 'My god, what did they do to you down there? They're a bunch of butchers in there!' You can imagine what I felt like, these doctors looking at me, saying a bunch of butchers had been at me.

It was awful, I think it's like having your womb taken away, you know, I was only 29, and they said, 'if it's spread we'll have to take both your testicles', I was just out of it. And I really regret not talking to people but I didn't know how to do it then and I can now but I could never have done something like that then. I was a very introverted person, I think I was like a lot of men, men find it difficult to talk and that changed me, you know, because my father was like, you know, you never discussed these things, you kept it to yourself.

Dr Goldblatt and I had disagreements about art and why I was doing it. He thought I was just doing it to better myself, to get on. I could understand where he was coming from, it was like my grandmother in a way, but I think he was missing the real point about me. There are all sorts of things I didn't understand at the time when I was having the therapy. I didn't understand some of the things he said because he didn't say very much, you do all the talking and then he says these crucial things to get you to think about. In a funny sort of way that was a bit like Zen, because you have to fill it in. Like trying to understand about the letting go business, it's not a conscious thing, it's got to be built-in so it's just a reflex in the end.

It's all those koans. My favourite is the one where the student has a problem with a woman and the Zen master says 'you know she's gone but you're still hanging on to her' the woman at the river edge. I did find therapy itself a bit like that, I had to think about it, and maybe if you're with a grandmaster it's different, but I was reading it out of a book and going to the Buddhist Society.

Chapter 7 - First Marriage, St Ives and Cambridge 1972-76

After Maxie and I got married we moved to St Ives in Cambridgeshire. She'd talked me into giving up my therapy at the Tavistock Institute under Dr Goldblatt. He wasn't too happy about that. He said he thought I needed longer, but he also said 'you've got the basic stuff to work on'. When I was going there I was quite interested in what he was saying and he obviously was helping me but there was a bit of resistance in me and I couldn't help but think 'perhaps it is all a load of rubbish really'. But it was after I'd stopped that I realised that he had definitely helped me and then I got interested in reading about Freud and Jung and Laing. I think he did give me the basis of understanding about myself where I could actually help myself from then on, so life changed drastically from being as I said before manic-depressive.

When we moved to St Ives we lived in a three-storey townhouse. It was an end terrace and very nice. It had a basement which had obviously been a shop, possibly a butcher's because it had hooks like meat hooks hanging from the ceiling. You went downstairs to the shop then up about five or six stairs to the front door which led into the living room and then there was the kitchen which you went downstairs to which overlooked the back garden. There were two bedrooms on the top and you went downstairs over the kitchen to the bathroom which had a very beautiful view of the River Ouse at the back. We had two rooms in the basement which used to flood when the River Ouse went up, but we didn't know that at first.

My wife was pregnant when we moved in and she fell through the kitchen floor as soon as we bought it so I had to rush about and get a load of timber. I was pretty naive because I'd never done a house up, I'd only painted things white and I didn't really know much about how you go about it. I went off to the second-hand place, and the guy was a real con-artist because he said 'oh this wood is brand-new you can sand it down and it'll make a nice floor '. What he didn't tell me was that it was what they call wet timber and it would shrink. I laid the floor and it gradually shrank so there was a huge gap. It wasn't tongue in groove, which it should have been. There were large gaps and because the kitchen was raised up a bit and it had air bricks underneath, when there was a wind from a certain direction it almost used to lift my wife's skirt. We put lino down, but even the lino used to rise up and go down in certain places so that wasn't very good.

But the house itself was a lovely house. It had a beautiful Georgian staircase and I don't know why it had such a beautiful one because the shop in the basement suggested it most probably was a tradesperson's house.

We had a very long garden with vegetables, and I built a studio in the garden out of brick. Laura, my step-daughter, went to the school in St Ives, it was quite nice to take her and I did do a bit of work there. I made a couple of pieces; I must have made *Table for One* there and *Chair*. *Chair* was about the ergonomics of sitting down, it was to do with an exercise they gave us at St Martin's in the first year. Caro gave us these exercises to do, like 'take a line for a walk' so you take a line for a walk from a line into a plane into a volume, these are very sort of Bauhausian art school projects. But one he got us to do was to make a piece of sculpture about somebody sitting down. I suppose the obvious would be somebody sitting on a chair but I suddenly thought, well, what happens when you sit down, how is the volume distributed? I learned how to bend some wood under steam so I had two curved pieces with a sort of seat on it, and then I made this plaster shape which went over the seat like your bottom might go over a very narrow seat. Caro thought it was good, and it stuck with me, so when I made *Chair* it wasn't so much the volume going over, it was the feeling of when you're standing with your back to the seat and you just let go to sit down. So actually the 'chair' I made has got no seat, it's just a triangle, because that's the ergonomics of suggestion.

I also made a couple of metal sculptures there which I haven't got any more, and I put up one which I did in the last one year of St Martin's which was a nice piece. I put that up in the garden but I haven't got it now, it was a very fragile piece made of aluminium and it sort of influenced me to make the pieces I did out of aluminium for *Table for One* and for *Chair* almost ten years later.

Then I found out my wife was very possessive and jealous. I had started work at the Cambridge College of Art and Technology (CCAT) and she was working in Peterborough Evening Institute and she was very very jealous of me working in the art school so our marriage began to crack-up.

Something else that contributed to the break-up was the problems with our son. When Simeon was born he died three times. He died once when she was giving birth to him so they had to get him out quick so he's still got forceps scars in his head. She was cut up quite badly getting him out so she was in hospital in bed for a long time. He was put in an incubator because he was two months premature. He was born at seven months and his lungs hadn't developed for him to breathe. There was a royal couple who had a child who had the same thing at the same time as this and that was in all the papers. The lungs weren't developed and it is a problem with children born at seven months that their lungs haven't developed enough. This wasn't related to her falling through the floor. She had had miscarriages twice to my knowledge before.

I'd invited my painter friend Paul up from London, and she had a drop too much red wine I think and that evening she was taken in to hospital by the doctor. She had what was termed a miscarriage because at seven months it's not a birth because the baby can't properly breathe, so he was put in an incubator with a sensitive blanket underneath him. They put him on a sensitive blanket and what used to happen was he would fall asleep and stop breathing, and every time he stopped, you come along lift the lid of the incubator and tickle the bottom of his feet and that gets him to breathe again, it was quite simple really. Years afterwards when my mother had died and I started really talking to my Dad, guess what, he was born at seven months, they didn't have an incubator in that period but they used to do the same thing to him, they used to tickle the bottom of his feet when he stopped breathing. It was quite strange really, but he never told me anything about this at the time my son was going through it.

After a couple of days she was allowed to come up and see him but I was with him all the time, I used to stay there. My mother had come up to look after Laura so I was at the hospital most of the time with him and I got rather emotional about it. There was one particular time I thought, well, I'd sooner sacrifice my own life for him so that he lived, it was most probably the only time in my life that I've actually prayed and really believed in it. But then when I went back to her bed she would say things like 'oh, he's my son, he'll survive'. She didn't seem to have any sense of reality about the situation as this little boy was fighting for his life. So it wasn't that we were falling out but I just felt it was an unreal situation.

The next thing that happened to him was that all the babies in the hospital got yellow jaundice and they didn't have enough ultraviolet lights to go round. These ultraviolet lights, which they're supposed to have if they get yellow jaundice, are like strip lights but they're in a curve, you need a whole set of them to go over one incubator . They had so many babies in there they didn't have enough lights, so they took the babies out of the incubators and put them in trays because the trays were smaller so they could get two trays under one set of lights. The nurse that transferred him from the incubator to the tray forgot his sensitive blanket so the next thing that happened the doctor called for me and said that they'd actually found him blue, he had died and they'd resuscitated him and they said 'we think he'll be all right but he will be small and he will be slow at some things' which he has been, he's smaller than me. They'd done a lumbar puncture in his spine with a big syringe and drawn off some of the spinal fluid and that told them how much brain damage he'd got. The doctor said 'I don't think he's going to be backward in the sense of actual proper brain damage, he'll most probably be a boxer or something'. He told me in the kindest way, I suppose, that he had died. I remember seeing him when he was a little boy naked and the scar from the lumbar puncture was huge, like another bottom hole, and as far as I know he's still got quite a big indentation in his spine.

That really did upset me and I came back to my mother who was looking after my step-daughter and she was saying 'oh I've had such a hard time here today' she wasn't listening to a word I said. I felt so upset I went down the road into St Ives and there was a wine cellar, a really good one there just over the bridge and he sold excellent bottles of wine. In those days you could buy a bottle of Sauternes for absolutely nothing, nowadays it's very expensive, but I bought a bottle of vodka and came back and drank it on the settee without my mother even noticing, she was just rambling on about what her day had been like. That was typical, like when I saw my friend Peter die, it was no good trying to talk to either of my parents about anything serious because I think both of them, especially my mother, had a mechanism of just shutting things out if they didn't want to know.

Then he had another turn, but this time it wasn't so bad. I can't remember what caused it, they told me that he'd stopped breathing again, but luckily somebody had got to him in time. He was in the hospital for quite a long time, until he got to about 3 lbs 14 oz. When he came out he was very fragile and my wife by that time had just come out. We didn't break up then but it had left me with my doubts about her. I suppose I felt in a way she was a bit like my mother, she couldn't actually cope with any sort of real reality.

Then one day I came back late from college and she was burning everything in a suitcase that I had. She burnt all the letters, and there were letters from a relationship I'd had with a woman called Wendy Taylor who was a sculptor at St Martin's, she burnt all her letters and photographs. She burnt the photographs of my Austin Champ, the jeep I had. She burnt letters from my friend Lizzie who was a poet, anything that happened before her she just took out of this suitcase and burnt. And when I got home she was just on the last bit of burning.

That really did it for me. I thought, I can't live under this 'where have you been, you're ten minutes late' regime so I left. I didn't leave with the intention of breaking up the marriage, I suppose at that point I was just trying to say 'look we've got to sit down and talk about it' because every time I tried to sit down and talk about it, she wouldn't burst into tears, but she would just be very aggressive with me so I thought well the only way is to leave.

It was May time and I'd just finished work at college and I wasn't being paid for the holidays. I started work as a painter and decorator for a subcontractor, I used to paint flats they were putting up in Cambridge, and get so much an hour. I literally lived on a friend's floor, his name was Alan Boyce, he was teaching three-dimensional design and he lived with his wife and his two children in Cambridge. I lived with him for about two months or something and I suppose his wife was trying to bring Maxie and me back together, but it didn't work, and just before the Christmas I got a letter from her solicitor saying that I'd committed adultery and she was divorcing me. The funny thing is I hadn't committed any adultery, that was too much for me and I thought well blow this I'm not going back. It was a silly move because I didn't really think about Simeon, because Simeon was going to be the problem and it was pretty nasty.

I had a friend I was seeing called Deborah and in the February we started an affair. I went to live with Simon Young, another friend who was teaching three-dimensional design and then when I found my own flat in about the March of the following year Deborah moved in with me. We had a flat in Cambridge, so that put paid to everything then, and so I went to a solicitor. She said 'well do you want a divorce or not?' and I said 'yes' so we agreed to go ahead on the grounds of adultery. Maxie had already sold the house by this time and moved to Brighton. She'd sent me a letter to say 'for the children's sake, so Laura can stay at St Ives school, will you sign over the house to me'. I signed over the house, didn't get anything for the house at all, and I found out afterwards, she'd already sold it by that time, and moved to Brighton. That meant I had to travel all the way from Cambridge down to Brighton to see my son and she was very difficult about it, so that ended up in a court case because a couple of times I went down there and they weren't in. We'd prearranged it and she was just being difficult, it was her way of getting back at me because she hadn't got a relationship and I'd started to make a new one.

When I started teaching at Cambridge College of Arts and Technology (CCAT) I found, as at Croydon, that there was a huge tradition of having plants in the art school, lots of plants on the landing so they could grow up to about 12 or 13 foot tall. John Boland, who was a Quaker, was head of the art school, and encouraged plants. There was a technician called Johnny Fisher from Cockermouth, whose job it was to look after the plants, and he was quite an interesting character himself. He was like my father, one of a big family, and all his brothers had had to go down the mines and he was determined not to. He ended up as a technician for the art school, he was quite a lively character to say the least, and when he retired from being a technician we brought him back to model because he had quite a good physique.

When I got to Cambridge I went to Kettle's Yard House, that was another influence on collecting glass things and having things with light coming through them. I liked the idea of etched glass and the way the whole house of Jim Ede is sorted out. Jim Ede lived there, it's his house you go and see, and he also worked at the Tate Gallery.

I worked on a lot of things to try and bring the city council and the college together. I tried to get a space in Cambridge with the council where artists could have studio space. That fell through because there just wasn't anybody on the council who was that enthusiastic and they maintained they'd had one years ago and it had got used and abused by all sorts of students from the art school and Cambridge University having parties and things but that's not what I had in mind anyway, I wasn't having it in mind for students at that time, but for professional artists' studios and a Centre for Artistic Endeavour.

I then started work on something called CAF, Cambridge Art Forum or Cambridge Art Factory, which was run by myself and a guy called Derek Batty. Derek Batty at that time was teaching art history at Cambridge School of Art and we ran this thing but, as people do, we fell out over whether it should be more a factory, more practice-based rather than theory-based. It ran for a year or two and it was good and we did a lot of talks and experimental things with other artists as well as students, it was open to everybody. We had a lot of problems getting studio space but in the end we used a school room.

After I parted from Maxie I was living in quite a small rented bedsit in Cambridge, and that's where I made *Window*. The flat was over a dentist's repair place, not a dentist it was a dental laboratory. It only had two rooms, we lived in one and I used one as a studio, so it's amazing that I managed to make *Window* there. I carried on with my observational drawings. I was so shocked about how dark and awful the first ones were when I was at Grange Road that I was determined to get my drawing back to the sort of standard it was when I was at Croydon because I hadn't been doing it regularly and it had deteriorated. So I carried on doing my tree drawings and I was friendly with another lecturer from Cambridge School of Art, Nicholas Barnham, who did boats and trees, so we used to go out drawing together when I wasn't making sculpture. Because making sculpture was such an intense psychological exercise for me it was nice just to go out and see something in front of me and just try to draw it.

Often it echoed things, like the *Lattice* pieces which I made later, when I was living in Farm Cottage, and which obviously came from sunlight coming from the trees. There were echoes, everything fed into everything, but to me at the time it felt that I was quite fragmented because I was doing paintings at the same time as I was doing sculpture and I was going out and doing these observational tree drawings. But in fact they were all the same problems in a way, and in Zen terms they were a good discipline, the whole discipline of having something there and having to interpret it.

I spent a lot of time with Nick and he had an agent in Hamburg who came and saw my stuff and said that he would sell mine too, mostly my tree drawings. So we used to go off to Germany, and I remember the first trip because Nick had got six children. He had a Volkswagen Caravette, mine had gone defunct years before, but he'd borrowed a Volkswagen Caravette from a friend and decided to put all his paintings in there to take them to this exhibition, and he would put some of mine in there as well. So we'd got these two lots of paintings, but at the time it there was a law in this country that if paintings or sculpture left this country you must fill out all these forms and get permission. Obviously this was geared for things like Rembrandts or Picassos leaving the country, it wasn't really intended for the likes of us, but we couldn't be bothered with all this bloody procedure so we had to hide the stuff under blankets and things. On top of that he'd got six kids, now the rule of the boat was you could take one vehicle I think with five passengers, so me and one of the kids I think had to hide under the blankets to get on the boat through customs. It was fine and then we had a problem at the other end because the German police decided that they were quite interested in this and we all looked like a bunch of hippies with long hair. They stopped us but luckily Sammy the German agent arrived just in time and talked to the customs officers.

Anyway we got through and that was the start of me showing my work in Germany. That was quite interesting, I had a couple of exhibitions in

Hamburg and one in Bonn. I can't remember now if I had one in Cologne but it was quite an interesting time and I met a lot of interesting people, including Albrecht, who bought some of my drawings. Albrecht was a lawyer in the German government but to do with the European Union and he was based in Bonn. Bonn was a very strange place, I liked Cologne but I didn't like Bonn very much, very provincial I think for a capital, as it was then, but Hamburg was an interesting place and Sammy was very friendly.

Sammy was quite a strange little person, he was quite short, very methodical and an incredible timekeeper. He used to drive me and Nick mad because he would say 'right, I'm going to unpack the car for ten minutes then I shall go to the toilet and in three minutes I should be back' and he did everything by the clock. I couldn't get my head around it but when you've known him for about eight years as we did you get used to it. Nick still knows him but I got so fed up with this in the end.

He invited me over to Hamburg several times and acquired some of my drawings. He lived in this beautiful flat overlooking the Alster, a big artificial lake in the middle of Hamburg. I remember the first time he took me to Hamburg and he said 'well I'll show you everything'. It was in January, it was freezing cold, something like 8° or 9° below zero, but it was that dry cold that you get in Germany and Poland, it wasn't this damp we get over here.

He took me out at night, and first of all we called at the station, then he called over a young boy and was talking to this young boy, and he said 'that's a rent boy'. Then he took me off to the back of the station where there were these ladies with fur coats on but with nothing on underneath in this freezing weather. I must admit they were quite attractive young ladies in a sort of Playboy way, beautiful figures and everything. But then he took me down to the docks which was like something from the paintings of George Grosz. We're talking about women that are just as wide as they are tall with moustaches and huge busts, very strange looking women often with short hair as if they'd come out of the 1930s. These were prostitutes for the sailors, they were in a way halfway between men and women, very odd, and that was him showing me the night life of Hamburg.

One time when I was there he took me to a pub that stayed open all the way through the night, maybe it stayed open for the people who were working for the port, I don't know what it was but it was an interesting pub.

It had these very long tables, a sort of bierkeller. There was a chap playing the piano, I was mesmerised by him, he was playing the sort of tunes that Marlene Dietrich or somebody would have sung, and more modern stuff, but it was just the way he was playing and his mannerisms.

Some football fans came and joined our table and started crying in their beer because their team had just lost. It was a really strange place and the thing with a bierkeller is, you have your pint of beer then you have a schnapps then your pint of beer and so on. We got there at three o'clock in the morning and by seven o'clock Sunday morning we couldn't stand up, me and Sammy and we had to get back to the flat.

It was between Christopher Isherwood and George Grosz's paintings and there were some very strange women in there and some very strange men and then these football players and a lot of workers off the docks. I was a bit worried because it was a bit loud, but there was no aggression, there were a couple of times it was a bit wild and everybody got louder. Sammy was enjoying it, he was in his element.

He was a very strange guy, his flat was strange and still is presumably. He insisted you had to leave the toilet door open when you were using it so that the cat could get to the litter tray. He'd got the biggest collection of b-novels, all the worst novels in the world, he'd made a collection of them. He had nothing there which you could call a classic, no Sartre, no Camus, nothing like that, I looked and couldn't see anything I recognised. He had this mad obsession that he used to go every Christmas morning to a little theatre near the lake where they used to do a German version of that Agatha Christie play, the one that's been going forever in London, *The Mousetrap*. He took me to it and I thought, God this is the dullest Christmas morning I've ever had in my life! It was awful, specially being in German. But anyway Sammy and I did go on for quite a long time, and he was quite good at getting rid of pictures for Nick and myself and trying to help us, but he was also a bit of a liability in lots of ways.

Chapter 8 - Farm Cottage 1976-82

In the end I managed to see Simeon and I used to have him in the school holidays, every Easter, Christmas and summer, so it wasn't too bad. After about six months of living in the flat I thought, well this is not such a good place to have him, so I put an ad in the Cambridge Evening News saying 'artist wants place to live in and doesn't mind doing it up'. I was contacted by a guy who owned a big estate on the Suffolk/Essex border. He had a four-bedroom cottage at Baythorn End which had holes right the way through the walls, and he said he'd give me two years free rent and I could live there and do it up. It was beautiful, really beautiful, idyllic and it had a Rayburn. It taught me such a lot about the countryside. I always liked being in the country anyway but it was a mile up off the road on this big estate.

He had very little agriculture, most of it was a head of 50 cattle, and because he had hunts and shoots he kept all the coppices, so it was an excellent place for me and Simeon. Simmy saw a calf being born, things like that, and it was lovely. It was about 30 to 40 minutes drive from there to the college along the Haverhill road, quite a notorious stretch of road, but I did that for about six or seven years.

I started to make quite a lot of sculpture once I got down there. I made *Thought* which was a very complicated piece of sculpture about the structure of thought and sort of abstract which I haven't got now. I made some very odd pieces of sculpture while I was in the cottage. By about 1981-82 I'd made *Lattice,* which was an abstract construction. In those days the acrylic sheet used to come with paper on it and instead of peeling the paper off I cut criss-cross lines and then took some pieces of the paper off and left pieces on so it had this lattice pattern all over. Not only did you have a piece of sculpture with a lattice pattern but when the light came through you had the pattern of the shadows. I've still got the first lattice piece I did but unfortunately the second one, which was the best, got very badly damaged in somebody's garage because it got wet and the paper was damaged, and it also got broken. I've still got it in my workshop, and I think it is really quite a good piece, one of the best pieces I've made, but it is very badly damaged. So I started with this idea of leaving paper on or putting stuff onto the acrylic itself in the 1980s, and I am still using that now with the *Codices* and other things I'm working on, so that was quite an important experimental step for me.

I was showing at a lot of East Anglian galleries like the Minories in Colchester, the Houswell Gallery, and Digswell Arts Trust. I showed in Cambridge at Churchill College so it was quite good and I suppose it was quite a relaxing time. The work wasn't too heavy at CCAT, so it was idyllic.

There were lots of ponds and things on the farm so if I got bored making sculpture I went out and did a lot of tree drawings. I'm quite fascinated by trees, I think it has something to do with the discipline I've got from reading Zen when I was in my twenties and I wanted to be able to draw trees exactly and show the structure of them and the way that they're worked out, because all trees are different.

When I'd first started teaching at CCAT, I'd met Mike Gillespie who was already teaching sculpture there one day a week. He taught at St Albans School of Art, but he also had a fractional appointment to teach one day on the foundation at CCAT. He became a really good friend, we used to discuss bronze casting which is what he took the students for.

When he found out that I'd moved to Baythorn End he said, 'you must go and see an old friend of mine called Daphne Herrion, she lives not far from you'. She lived in a village called Sturmer on the outskirts of Haverhill, on a beautiful farm all on her own. She had the most amazing studio there which was attached to the house.

Daphne was a sculptor who was very prominent in the 1950s, a figurative artist and she worked in clay. Her maiden name was Hardy, Herrion was her husband's name and he was involved in the Festival of Britain. She had an affair with Arthur Koestler and I think that's how she found herself on her own. There's a piece of her sculpture at Addenbrooke's Hospital in Cambridge, I don't think that's a particularly good piece actually, but she did do some good pieces. She was quite good at drawing too, I've got a photocopy of a portrait that she did of me.

She was a really interesting personality. I met her and instantly we got on in a very strange way. She didn't like the girlfriend I was living with at all, she used to say: 'What are you living with her for, she's absolutely hopeless and she's a child, she's half your age!' Well she wasn't actually half my age at all, I wasn't that old!

When I went round there she always gave me things to do. She had artichokes and things that she was growing and a couple of times I went round there and there was a tramp. He was a real tramp, he wasn't like people that live in caravans, this guy used to trudge around the country with a backpack. He slept in a barn, she gave him cups of tea and I think she found him interesting.

Daphne was a sort of old-school interesting personality herself. I would go round there, knock on the window and watch her. She used to be modelling on her stand, clay modelling with a fag hanging out of her mouth, just like my grandmother. There was always a fag hanging out the corner of her mouth with a long ash on, and she used to drink quite a lot if I remember, there was always wine when I went round there.

Farm Cottage was lovely, but by the early 1980s I was thinking about trying to purchase a property of my own. I needed a building where I could have my work secure. I had about £5000, and I looked around the whole country to see what I could buy and I couldn't come up with anything. Other than some terraced houses in South Wales where the ground had been mined underneath, there was nothing going up for sale at that sort of price.

Then in 1982, Simon Young, a great friend of mine and fellow teacher at CCAT who I've mentioned before, bought an old derelict chapel - I think it was a Methodist or Baptist chapel - near Stamford in Lincolnshire. So he gave me the idea of having a look round, and I started looking where the Church Commissioners advertised, I think it was in the London Gazette.

There were two churches that the Church Commissioners were selling, one for £5000 in East Heckington which is 8 miles south-west of Boston and there was one on the outskirts of Horncastle. Simon came up to see both of them with me and he said 'well I think the one near Boston is much more serviceable'. It was about a two hour drive either up the A604 as it was then and then up the A1 and across from Stamford, or up the A10 to King's Lynn and then across from King's Lynn onto the Boston Road , and the Sleaford Road, and that took two hours where the Horncastle one would have taken at least two and a half, it was too far out so that was one problem. I took photographs of both buildings but unfortunately I haven't got photographs of the other one near Horncastle as far as I know.

I chose Lincolnshire because it was cheap. These were substantial buildings, they weren't going to fall down. And for £5000 it was enormous, 50-80 foot long, by 30 foot wide, and if you weren't bothered about the architecture you could have got three floors in there, but I only got two because I didn't want to go through the windows.

It was a substantial Victorian building that was built in about 1896 for the overflow of Heckington. This was when they needed lots of agricultural workers, so this was a village that had been made for the overflow. They put up a church and a school to go with it, and it had a vicarage on one side of the church. It was on a third of an acre with a drive of about 80-100 feet with a nice wrought iron gate and then up the drive were ten yew trees. Also the graveyard was all round the Church, but when I bought it the Church Commissioners said that I could fence off the main graveyard and dispense with the graves that were around the church because they had notified the relatives and no one had objected.

Debbie, my girlfriend at the time, who was living with me at Farm Cottage, worked as an occupational therapy nurse and put up some of the money for the church. She never lived there because there was nowhere for us to live. We just used to go up there and come back. I bought an old caravan for about £50 I think but it served the purpose, we could stay over there on Saturday and Friday nights when we came up from Suffolk. Deborah came up a few times and helped me clear the garden, all the nettles and things, because it was just nettles everywhere.

However, not long after we'd bought the church, I met someone else and my relationship with Debbie broke up. She stayed in Farm Cottage and I virtually moved into the caravan, but she had a financial interest in the church and of course she wanted her money back, and although it wasn't very much money, I didn't have any money at all. She got it in the end, I had to raise it, but she did decide to annihilate my big sculptures in the garden, she broke up about five big aluminium sculptures.

That was a really bad thing because I didn't even know they'd been destroyed. I hired a lorry to go and pick them up and they weren't there and I didn't know what to do because I'd negotiated with her to come down that day. She knew I was coming down to pick them up and they weren't there, so I thought they'd been stashed away in a barn or something. I had a good look round, but in the end I gave up, and as I was driving back I saw her walking along the road. She was very reluctant to get in the lorry because she had to tell me where they were. She'd obviously sold them for scrap. I was really upset about it because there were one or two really good pieces, which could never be made again, I've got pictures of them.

So that really did finalise that relationship, because as you know, you don't just stop a relationship, it sort of peters out over time, but that just about annihilated it. I was shocked that I'd lived with somebody for seven years, they knew the value of my work, they knew how much time I put into it, they knew that I didn't get much for it, and they could just bring in people and destroy it. I realised that she must have been incredibly bitter and I hadn't seen that in her at all. So that finalised that.

My new girlfriend, Fiona, like a lot of people when they get in a new relationship, she didn't want to know, I mean you don't want somebody sitting there talking about their past relationship do you? Daphne was the only one that I could talk to and she said 'well you must do something about it, you can't just let her get away with it' she said 'because okay, you've left her, but you haven't done her any harm, you're going to pay her the money for the church, go to the police'.

I went to the police in Suffolk the following day and they weren't at all interested. 'Oh well what's this rubbish' as soon as I showed them the photos 'oh it's the best thing for it ha ha'. I thought 'I'm not getting anywhere here'.

Daphne put me on to a solicitor in Cambridge and she said 'why should you pay her for the church now when she's just broken up five sculptures that could be worth a lot more than that'? because I owed her about two and a half thousand for her share of the church.

So I got a solicitor and there was a court case over it. In court cases like that, you have to get somebody who values the works of art and then they get somebody who values the works of art and the judge wasn't sympathetic. I knew I was in for it because he started off the proceedings by saying 'oh, I'm a watercolour artist, let's see these lovely sculptures' and of course when he saw them he obviously thought 'what rubbish is this?' and then proceeded to tell me what a bad boy I'd been for having so many girlfriends.

He awarded me the value of the materials, that's all, off the price of the church, and then after we came out she said it was a really good relationship and I said, 'well, you can say that, but for a relationship with an artist, for you to destroy his work, you can't have ever expected it to have worked'. Sometimes, like with my first wife, you come back together again, but that sort of finalised everything. I mean I'm not going to go with somebody who destroys my work.

At about the same time as I bought the church and changed girlfriends, Daphne went to live in Cambridge at Owlstone Road in Newnham. She was living in much smaller accommodation, a beautiful house, it was sort of Edwardian with a nice little garden. She had a studio shed at the bottom of the garden. Fiona and I used to come down from the church and stay with her. Daphne was very helpful to me when I needed somewhere to stay, because we couldn't afford to pay rent anywhere, because I was quite destitute at that time, and Fiona was out of work, and it took about five years of work on the church before we could live in it.

There was a bookcase in the room we were staying in at Daphne's, and Fiona found the love letters between Daphne and Arthur Koestler amongst the books and read them. I wouldn't do that so I don't know what was in them and Fi never told me before she left, so I've no idea, which is a shame really because it would have been interesting. I think there were a lot of them because she took a long time reading them, but I just felt I couldn't do anything like that, it's much too private. I'm not sure whether Daphne knew that she was reading them. They had this sort of antagonistic relationship, and maybe Fi could have read them to get back at her, or just out of curiosity or on the other hand Daphne could have given them to Fiona to read, especially as I found out that Daphne's bark was worse than her bite.

Chapter 9 - The Church

There were two churches I was interested in buying, the one made out of brick at East Heckington, which was the one I eventually bought, and the stone one. The brick one was frost damaged on the north facing wall. It had been left derelict and the guttering had all come down, it hadn't had a gutter for at least 10 or 15 years, so the water had run off the outer wall and gone onto the brick and then being north facing in the middle of winter it had frozen on the brick and brought about half an inch of the bricks away, not all over the wall but over about a third. I took photographs and went down to see my father, because he had been a bricklayer. I showed him the photos and he came up and had a look at it. When he'd seen it he said 'no it's not a big problem we can repair this'.

I really preferred the other one because it was a beautiful little stone church, but unfortunately when it had been built in the Victorian era they had done the mortar between the stones far too hard with concrete. The mortar has to be softer than the stone itself, because when the mortar is too hard, instead of the water running out through the mortar it gets held in the stone and when the frost comes it expands and pieces break off. The stone church was quite bad all the way round at a low level. If you can imagine a block of stone 10-15 inches wide and half of it breaking off, you would have had to jack up the whole building to get that stone out to put another piece of stone in. This is what had happened to the one I bought as well, but it wasn't so bad, and my father was able to repair the whole north wall for me, whereas you couldn't have repaired the stone church without vast sums of money.

I was rather disappointed in the other one because it was a very beautiful church and it was a Grade 1 listed building. I often wondered whether I was making a wise decision buying the one at East Heckington, because it was nice but it wasn't so pretty and the other one was very pretty with a square belfry, whereas the one I bought had a typical Lincolnshire shiplap belfry, octagonal supported by the roof with a spire on it.

One day when Fiona and I were working on the church we went to see what had happened to the other one, and it wasn't there. The Church Commissioners had pulled it down, even though it was a Grade 1 listed building. Years later they got criticised for doing it, but one of the things I didn't know until we bought the church was that they could do whatever they liked. The solicitor in Cambridge who dealt with it for me, said 'it's amazing because they're beyond the law, nobody else would be able to pull down a Grade 1 listed building'. I was disappointed that it had gone because it was a beautiful building.

It took about a year to buy the church, because it was very complicated, I had to submit plans to the Church Commissioners and negotiate over what they would allow. Obviously they didn't want me to do anything that changed the nature of the building, but they had some funny ideas themselves. In the nave there were ten tall leaded-light windows and I was going to put in roof lights, but they suggested that I put in dormer windows. Well that wouldn't have worked, dormer windows would have projected horribly beyond the roof, but I said I was going to put the roof lights in so they passed all the plans. Then I had to subject the plans to the local authority, and I made friends with Mary Kerr, the listing officer who came to the church and listed it as a building of special interest, and her husband, Nigel. Nobody had been interested in it until I bought it, it had lain there for ten years and some of the stained glass windows had been damaged, not smashed, but people had been taking pot-shots with air rifles and putting holes through them.

I went to Lincoln and spoke to the Clerk of the Works, a nice man called Mr Day, to find out about why the stone butts around the stained glass window were weathering away, and it was he who told me about the really hard mortar that the Victorians used, that was causing the problem. I also talked to him about the stained glass and he pointed out that most probably some of the stained glass that was in the church was from much earlier. They used to move stained-glass around, so for example if somebody who had plenty of money in a village was willing to offer a new triptych at the end of the church, they would then take the existing stained-glass out and put the new one in, and take that off to somewhere else. So you can see that our attitude of preciousness towards cathedrals and churches is all very well but on a low level it didn't always work like that, and I realised that it has probably only come about in the last hundred years or so. There were different periods of stained-glass in the chancel, including a very beautiful single long stained-glass window that was dedicated to a young girl who had died, sort of Art Nouveau/Art Deco, and that was done very nicely.

There were a lot of things in the church which took a lot of time to do. It sat on a third of an acre and had a drive of about 80 feet with five yew trees on each side, 10 yew trees up the drive. It had all the gravestones left on the right-hand side with permission that the parish council would come and take those grave stones away. They never did, I had to remove them myself in the end, I kept on to them but they never came. That made the garden but it was full of nettles so they all had to be dug up by hand. And then on the left side I made the vegetable plot. There were quite a few trees, Irish yew around the church and loads of pine. The main graveyard at the back was accessed by a footpath, it came across my property but luckily it was at the side so that wasn't a problem.

The Church Commissioners wanted me to buy the whole graveyard, but the local parish council wouldn't hear of it because it was still being used. In the graveyard around the church, the bit I'd bought, everything was over 50 years old. If it's over 50 years old and the Church Commissioners get in touch with the relatives and they give permission for them to be removed it's okay, and that's what they did, so I was allowed to take them up.

Some of the gravestones in the main graveyard were only 5 or 10 years old, but that wasn't part of what I'd bought. It was a mess, full of waist high nettles except for one tiny little plot where the family came every Sunday. I don't know what their original nationality was, whether they were from the fens or whether they'd moved there from elsewhere at some time, but they looked after their parents' and their brothers' and sisters' graves and that was the only bit of the churchyard which was ever cultivated.

I complained to the parish council about all the nettles. I'd cleared my patch but the graveyard was full of nettles and they were just spreading in every time I cleared them from the garden. So I got onto the parish council and said 'look this won't do because I'm trying to make a garden here'. I said 'if you won't let me buy it then at least you could clean it up' because I'd made a path on the side of my property with a separate gate so people could still walk over my property. I'd actually bought the land, but it was a public right of way to the graveyard and I didn't mind that, they didn't interfere with me and I didn't interfere with them and they didn't overlook anything.

Then the parish council brought in a local agricultural worker who just sprayed petrol all over the graveyard and set the whole thing alight, so all the nettles went but all gravestones were scorched. I made an enemy there because I complained to the Church Commissioners and they never did it again. I don't know what happened between them but I felt it was disgraceful really, this lack of respect for the people that had been buried in the graveyard. The local church was supposed to come and remove the gravestones and they never did so I removed them myself. The parish council wouldn't have anything to do with it, other than try and set the whole bloody place alight. It was up to the local diocese, and they didn't want to do anything either, so I stood the gravestones up when I removed them, against one of the trees, there weren't that many huge gravestones but they were nearly 100 years old and that's where they were when I left, nobody bothered to do anything with them. I fenced off all the graves that were quite modern, none of them were actually on my property anyway because when the Church Commissioners drew up the plan of the ground they were quite sensitive to where new gravestones were and where they weren't.

When I bought the church, there was no water there, no electricity, no sewerage, so the first thing I had to do was get water and electricity because Fiona and I were living in a caravan in the drive. I don't know if you've ever lived in a caravan, but without electricity all you've got to get you through the winter is Calor gas, and you get terrible condensation, so when you wake up in the morning, especially in the cold, your bed's just full of water, it's hot inside but it's also incredibly wet. So the first thing I had to do was get electricity and water on. That meant digging a trench 1 foot 6 inches down to lay the water and electricity on. The problem with that is that I'd got ten protected yew trees in the drive, so I couldn't just dig a trench all the way the 50 or 60 feet. What I had to do was literally dig the trench, get down in the trench, and tunnel under the roots of the trees in some places. It took me about two months to do this, and then once I'd got electricity on I could have an electric fire in the caravan, and that kept it warm and dry.

And then the next part was the sewerage. Because there was no mains sewerage, you had to have the septic tank 50 feet away from the building, with a 50 foot run-off. The length of the drive was 80 feet, so I had to do the same with that, I had to tunnel some of it under the roots, to the septic tank.

The church occupied a lot of my time, because I was doing all the building work myself. One of the first jobs I had there was the belfry, because it was completely rotten so I had to get up on the tower and renew the octagonal belfry and take down the spire. Until I got the church I was terrified of heights, it sort of got me over that because I hadn't got the money to bring in builders and I either got up there and did it myself or I just abandoned the whole project.

It appears I was the laughing stock of the village, and there was a bit of comedy in it. I got up into the octagonal building and took the bell down because I was frightened that with all the rot the bell would fall on my head. It was a big bronze bell, I managed to get that down the scaffolding but then I realised that the actual steeple had to come down.

I got up into the belfry and I thought, well, I need some sort of safety device so I tied a very thick rope about an inch diameter round my chest and around the strong pillars of the belfry while I tried to get a ladder up balanced on the ridge up the steeple, and of course the more I moved the tighter the rope became round my chest. The whole village was watching this with glee because some of them were pretty antagonistic towards me, being an outsider. In the end I had to get rid of the rope because it was causing me more trouble than it was worth. Of course looking from the ground the steeple didn't look all that big but in fact it was very large.

Tea With Douglas

The man who'd bought the school next door had a friend who was an electrician and he said, 'There's only one way to get that down Douglas, you've got to saw through the main supports of the steeple and topple it over the side of the building' rather like you'd topple a tree. He said 'I'll come up and help you' which he did and the two of us toppled it, and on the top of the steeple was what looked like a little cross but it was about 8 foot to 10 foot long and it just stuck right in the ground, it was enormous.

That took me a year, and I built a small roof-cum-steeple with a weathervane. I built it down on the ground and took it apart and then reconstructed it up there, and the only way I could do it was to reconstruct it up there with me sitting on half of the octagonal bit of the belfry and having that resting on my knees and over the other half, and then pulling it over my head and bolting it all in place. Then I made doors and glazed the whole thing, because the problem with the octagonal belfry was that it was all open so I glazed it to stop the water coming in. The roof was a scissor-jack roof and that had badly decayed under the belfry. The rest of the roof was fine, it was just underneath, these things were about 12 inches deep and I had to cut out about 2 inches with woodworm.

It took about another year for Fiona and I to do the chancel and the vestry. The nave, the big bit, was just studio, then there was the chancel and the vestry. We put in a mezzanine floor, so it wouldn't go through the stained-glass windows, and that was where we slept. Then I built a crude shower in the nave, you went for a shower in this freezing cold nave. The chancel became the living room and I put in a pot-bellied stove because there was a chimney there. There was a system for heating the church, a huge iron sort of oven, which circulated hot air through grates throughout the church. It was a Victorian invention and it was completely impractical because it would have used up so much fuel, obviously fuel was cheaper for churches in Victorian times. So I decided to get rid of this cast-iron thing, it was this about 4-5 foot big and about 3 foot wide and I got my little sledgehammer and hit it and it just bounced off. Then I hired a huge sledgehammer, brought it down on the roof of this thing and the head of the hammer just went flying off. The guy was very nice to me and lent me another one and in the end I managed to break it up. It was cast-iron and cast-iron is really hard to break up, it splinters and they fly off in all directions.

There were all sorts of problems with the church. One day quite soon after buying it there was a slate loose so I got my ladders out and got up on the roof and I was just about to slip this slate under the other slates when I was pushed flat against the roof, completely flat, by this awful air pressure, and then there was a horrendous noise. It was an American jet, they're not supposed to fly lower than 50 feet but it was certainly lower than that. I phoned them up and asked them first, and they said well it's got to be below 50 feet to push you against the roof. Then I wrote a letter and complained about it and they sent me a really nice letter back actually saying they didn't know that it was being used as living quarters, that as far as they knew it had been disused for over 10 years and they were just using it for practising flying close enough to a building to shoot at it. They weren't actually shooting at it, that was true, because you could see all the bullet holes in the stained glass had been shot from the other side, not the direction they came from. The way the air pellets had gone you could see that it was shot from the ground most probably by children. They were just practising low-level flying, and they admitted this in the letter and said they wouldn't do it again and they never did. They were quite nice about it, but it was frightening for me because funnily enough you don't hear the noise till the plane's gone, so first of all there was the air pushing me against the roof and then this horrendous noise. So there were lots of incidents about the church which were quite frightening I suppose.

We got back from me teaching in Cambridge one Friday night to find that a snowplough had come into the village. He thought the church wasn't being used so he'd put the whole of the snow in front of my gate so we couldn't even get in, we had shovel it all out to get into the drive where the caravan was.

Having the church gave me all the space I needed because the nave was about 50' x 30'. I made quite a lot of sculpture there, I made *Famine* and *Shelter* and a lot of pieces that were to do with the human condition and it culminated in an exhibition at the Trade Union Congress in London. It's a big building in Great Russell Street, not opposite the British Museum but not far down the road, and I quite liked that exhibition because I had to do everything myself, the posters, everything. I put on about seven or eight sculptures which all dealt with the human condition: *Famine*, *Table for One*,

Shelter, Hiroshima. I put in a lot of works that I'd made at the church about these kind of problems. I didn't get much feedback, but what I did get was good. I invited a few people from the press along but they either didn't turn up or whatever, but I got feedback from the trade union people themselves and that was enough.

I mentioned earlier that while I was living at the church I got friendly with Mary Kerr who was the listing officer who came round to list the church and her husband Nigel, who was training to be a vicar. We became good friends, especially in the period when I was on my own, after Fiona left and before I met my second wife, they were really the only friends I had in Lincolnshire. Mary and Nigel were writing a series of books on parish churches in Lincolnshire. Mary could do the architectural illustrations but she wasn't so good on the more figurative illustrations like the figures on the tombs, so I volunteered to help her with the figure sculptures and draw those for the book.

Nigel was a very strange character and he had his bad points, but he had his good points too, he was a very warm personality and he did try and help people. One of the people he came across was a young man called Stephen, a teenager who had osteoporosis very badly. He'd broken quite a lot of the bones in his body, and because of that the kids in the village where he lived were really nasty towards him, I suppose they thought he was some sort of runt or something. Sometimes you get those sorts of attitudes in very parochial country villages where they just pick on people. Nigel told me this horrendous story about Stephen being stoned by the children of the village. He lived in a caravan because his parents had thrown him out, so he was obviously a bit of a character and a bit of a problem but then to suffer from such severe osteoporosis must have affected him.

Nigel decided to help him and we found out he was incredibly good at drawing, so we got him to help with the book illustrations which really did boost his morale, and at the same time we tried to support him in other ways. He must have been about 17 I think because he was on unemployment benefit and they suddenly called him in and said he must take a job as a labourer. I remember Nigel and I accompanying him to the unemployment office and really having a lot of words with them about it and getting very angry because you can't expect a teenager who's suffering from osteoporosis to climb up ladders and carry bricks and things and they didn't really want to know, it was just unbelievable that this was the attitude in the 1980s.

I don't know what happened to him in the end because I lost touch with Nigel after I sold the church and moved down to Cambridge, so I lost touch with Stephen too because I didn't know where Stephen lived, I'd only met him when he was at Nigel's. But the last thing I heard about him was that he was going to go to art school and to get some sort of art training, so I hope things worked out for him.

Chapter 10 - Dublin and Barcelona 1987-88

After Fiona and I had been together for about four years, she decided she'd had enough of me and the church and left. I was stuck there on my own and that was quite difficult for me because I was very fond of her. I don't know what had happened, perhaps the passion had gone, but anyway things weren't working out

I came back to Cambridge and at that time I wasn't staying with Daphne but in another part of Newnham in a bedsit that Fi and I had rented. I think Fi and Daphne in the end didn't get on very well, but anyway we couldn't stay there for four years, we just stayed there for a limited time until we found our own place but all we could afford was a bedsit in rather a strange house which was full of dogs, I think they were red setters, I'm not sure, something like that. The landlady kept dogs and she rented out some of her house. I think she worked in the Chemistry Department at CCAT but she had an accident and left. She had an enormous scar from her wrist almost up to her shoulder, so obviously something awful had happened to cause it.

We never lived completely in the church, only in the three-month period during the summer or at Easter and at Christmas, and for extended weekends the rest of the time when I was teaching, but we didn't live there full-time when I was teaching because it was too far to commute. So we had the bedsit for two or three years and it wasn't great but it was okay. It was rather nice being in Cambridge and being able to cycle everywhere. I had lived in Cambridge before for a short period of time when my first marriage broke up, but mainly on the floors of friends, and I'd had another bedsit over a dentist repair shop, but I hadn't been in Cambridge for any length of time and we did live there on and off for about three years. It was quite nice to actually just cycle about and get to know Cambridge and we did really enjoy ourselves going to the Arts Cinema etc.

When Fi went I had the problem of coming back to the same place on my own and I remember coming back and feeling very miserable because I was finding it very difficult. I could do drawings in the bedsit but the only place I could really make sculpture was at the church and I didn't fancy going up there all on my own all the time. So I didn't do much work, there was a period of about two years when I did masses of drawings but very little sculpture. I'd already had the exhibition at the TUC on *Famine* and *Shelter* but I wasn't making any more sculpture.

I was teaching a student from Dublin and she said 'why don't you come over at Christmas and I'll meet you and show you Dublin. You might be able to get a gallery that's interested in seeing your work'. So I went over to Ireland during the Christmas break.

I wanted to go and see New Grange. New Grange is a prehistoric burial mound and there's a period at the Midwinter solstice when you can actually view the sun shining into the tomb if it's not cloudy. I'd just missed that by a couple of days, but they put on this electric light that shines in the tomb, and as I'd only missed it by a couple of days I thought I'd go anyway. I caught the coach from Dublin to County Meath and I got to the town, Drogheda, but then there was no way in those days of getting to the actual site, so I had to get a taxi. We're talking about 1987/88, the Northern Ireland thing is still going on, and I didn't think about it, I didn't realise how close it was to the border. The taxi driver was rather unfriendly, not very helpful, and it suddenly dawned on me, here I am, an English university lecturer going off to County Meath to see New Grange and here's this guy who most probably in his spare time belonged to the IRA or was sympathetic to them. So I just said to him 'it's nice to be in Dublin because my grandmother was born in Dublin' and that was it, then he was the friendliest man I've ever come across. He didn't actually wait for me, but he went off and came back to pick me up because there was no way for me to get back, and he took me for free all along the River Boyne, and of course that was where it all happened in the first place. He told me the whole history, and he was a very friendly man, but obviously he wanted to know whose side I was on and where my sympathies lay, and actually my sympathies have always been with the Republicans anyway. I couldn't bear Ian Paisley, when I used to see him on the television I used to think, 'god what an awful man, why is he given so much time on English TV?'

I also had an interesting time when I got back to Dublin because the student who'd invited me over introduced me to a very beautiful young lady who was very tall with red hair. Her father had a psychoanalysis business in New York and he had a big house in Phoenix Park which is the place to live in Dublin. He had all daughters as far as I remember and they were all very beautiful and I thought, 'well there's no chance for you Douglas, you're far too poor!' She invited me out to meet her father to look at some pictures that I'd got, I'd been doing some pastel drawings. He was quite interested in one but for some reason, I think it was my own fault, he never bought it I don't think I ever sent it to him. But I did notice that the things that were hanging on his walls were very very expensive paintings by people we all know, so he was obviously making a lot of money. After I came back, I signed up to go to a symposium on public art in Dublin that was due the following summer.

When Easter was coming around, my technician Steve, who was one of my ex-students, said 'why don't you go away on holiday? Have three weeks off and try and get over it' because I was still brooding over the break-up with Fiona. I said 'fine, but where?' and he said 'well you could go and visit my brother, he's got a flat in Barcelona.' So I said okay and Steve phoned him up and arranged it.

It was rather hilarious because he'd never mentioned anything about his brother other than that his brother would be willing to put me up. I arrived at this flat in Barcelona rather late. I got a taxi and the taxi driver took me there and dropped me off. I rang the outside doorbell, but nobody answered it. It wasn't cold, Barcelona is nearly always warm at Easter like a summer's day, so it was warm but I was just hanging around outside in the dark at eleven o'clock at night. Eventually a Spanish person came in who was obviously renting on one of the other floors and he let me into the block, but I couldn't get into the flat which was on the top floor. I sat down by the outside door of the flat and they all came home about one o'clock in the morning.

Steve's brother turned out to be a student at the college in Cambridge where I was teaching, and so did the people who were sharing the flat, there were about four or five of them all together. They were doing Spanish at CCAT with a guy called Tony Morgan who I knew vaguely. I was a bit embarrassed because here I was, a lecturer, 20 years older than them and they were putting me up, but actually they were wonderful. There was a young man called Chris and his girl riend Caroline who took me all over Barcelona and showed me everything. And within three or four days I was madly in love with Barcelona because it was such a beautiful place

I'd been abroad before but I hadn't been to a Mediterranean city and it was really lovely, having the sea there, and the Gaudis, I hadn't been anywhere like it. I came back thinking 'my god this was fantastic it was absolutely beautiful, I must go again'.

When I came back I saw my friend Mike Gillespie, the one who introduced me to Daphne Herrion, and he said 'my son's living in Barcelona in a flat it right in the middle of the city'. The place I went to the first time was called Sant Antonio, on a road called Florida Blanca, it was a beautiful district but it wasn't in the tourist centre. But Mike's son lived right off the Ramblas in a very old flat, again on the top floor of an old building. He said 'my son is going out with a Catalan lady and they've been living together in her flat and they both want to come over for three months to see me and go to the Edinburgh Festival. I'm sure they'd be willing to rent you this flat'. So in the summer I had three months of a flat in Barcelona all to myself, so I thought, though it didn't actually turn out like that.

I arrived at the flat and Nick, Mike's son, and his Catalan girlfriend Magda were there and I stayed a couple of nights with them before they left and got to know how the flat and everything worked. They said to me 'if you want to draw on the walls don't worry about it'. I think they regretted that because I did do some very mad drawings at the time and I don't think they were too pleased when they came back.

The flat was on a street called Carrer de Jovellanos. Jovellanos was a Spanish writer of the 18th-19th century. It was a really nice flat but it had its drawbacks and one of them was the water supply. When you went up into the roof for the four or five flats you had these big asbestos tanks on them and a piece of lead channelling on top of the asbestos with little grooves cut out of it. The water used to come along that groove and literally just drip into the tank, so if you used your supply of water in the tank then you'd have to wait a couple of weeks for it to fill up again. I'm not joking, this is the way old flats in Barcelona were, it was the old system of getting water to the buildings.

So I soon ran out of water but that wasn't exactly my fault. The first thing that happened was that I met some young ladies on the Ramblas who had nowhere to live. I think there were three or four of them. They didn't want to stay long, they were all Dutch, there was Dominique, Barbara and I can't remember the other one or the other two's names, but anyway I put them up. They had sleeping bags and of course being women they had no idea about water, so within about two days of them being there I had no water at all left in the tank which wasn't very nice because of course you couldn't even flush the toilet.

Then two friends of Nick arrived because they thought he was still there so I put them up, Tom and somebody else, I can't remember his name. They got on very well because they were about the same age as the Dutch girls, but luckily after about a week they all left and I had the place to myself.

One night I was just sitting there looking out of the window down into the street and there were three men breaking into the side windows of the parked cars in the street and helping themselves to whatever they could find. I watched them go down the whole row and I couldn't do a thing about it because I had no Spanish. We did have a telephone in the flat but I couldn't have done anything about it, I didn't know any Spanish people, I couldn't ring the police and explain, so I just watched. It was very strange to be out of it, very odd to be as if you weren't there, you were just an Observer watching this scene like it was on a film. I never quite understood why it was important at the time that I was an Observer but I realised many years afterwards that I'd often been an Observer, like my friend Peter dying and I couldn't do anything about it then because I was so young, I didn't know what to do and I didn't really understand about my own psychology.

One day there was a ring at the doorbell and somebody introduced himself as Pep, with his girlfriend Nuri. They were friends of Nick and Magda, and they came to ask if I was getting on all right. They were Catalan, and I started a friendship with them which has carried on to this day. I think Pep had gone to design school, they have design schools in Barcelona as well as art schools, and I don't know what Nuri was doing then but she later became an administrator to Barcelona University, the one on the Diagonal, and sadly she died of cancer a few years ago. I still miss her lovely smile.

We had some great times together, but they did take a lot of drugs and I found myself taking quite a few drugs myself. I limited it to cannabis, I didn't have to take anything else because I hallucinate on cannabis anyway. I remember lying there one night in my bed in the big double bedroom and watching these dinosaurs come in the door and knowing that it was an hallucination but enjoying it.

Over that period I did about 200 pastel drawings on paper and a lot of stuff came out. The only drawing I sold of that time, which I think is the best, was called *Alice and the White Rabbit*. There was always something for me about Alice and the white rabbit. When I lived with my grandparents my grandfather or grandmother must have read me the story because in their garden they had a lilac tree and I remember sitting under it and thinking 'oh there goes the white rabbit', as though I'd put myself in the story. For years afterwards I used to think 'oh I used to know the white rabbit and Alice' and my parents would look at me as though I was completely off my head.

But it was a very strange drawing that I did. It was Alice in the likeness of some photographs that the author had actually done of this young girl that I saw later on, she does look a bit like her and I don't think I knew of those photographs at that time. But the rabbit is a rather plump middle-aged man. He's just looking at Alice and she's looking at him. It's a very very strange drawing but I think it's quite a good one. I still haven't worked it out, it's something to do with my own psychology and the psychology of the story. I think it helped me, I think it worked something out of my system and I'm not quite sure even now what it was, there was something dating back from my childhood. It's a relationship of this young girl with this middle-aged man, actually that was almost the story itself wasn't it, if you read about Lewis Carroll?

In the middle of this three month stay in Barcelona I went to Ireland again to speak at a symposium on public sculpture and give a paper on public art, which they subsequently lost, so it was never published. Mine was the only one that wasn't published but they all said it was good. I met Eduardo Chillida there, the Basque sculptor. He opened the Symposium and he did these big metal sculptures, really good ones. Some of them are on the Basque coastline I think, or it maybe Galicia, and there's a particular piece, *Peine del Viento*, or *Wind Comb*, which overlooks the sea and looks very beautiful and I was interested in what he'd got to say. He was a completely different person to me but we got on really well. Then there was Albert Elsen, the art historian, who I also met and he'd written a lot on Rodin, Brancusi and the pioneers of modern sculpture and I'd always liked what he said. He gave a lecture on Rodin which cut across the lecture I gave a bit, because I started off with Rodin, but it didn't really make much difference because I was just talking about *The Burghers of Calais* in the context of the human condition and how I thought it was one of the best sculptures. He invited me to Stanford University in California to look him up.

At the same time in Dublin I met an old friend from St Martin's called Rudi Leeders and I made two new friends, Gerry Cox from Ireland and Stephen Hart from Australia. So it was a good time for meeting people including Andreu Arriola and Carmen Fiol, the architects who were instigating the change in Barcelona for the 1992 Olympics, because they came and gave a paper on public art. I also met Mary Bates from Sonoma State University who I was later to exchange with.

As I said, I'd been to Dublin the Christmas before when I went to New Grange, but it was completely different being shown around by people who really knew Dublin like Gerry. I was quite impressed by Trinity College, and O'Connor's Bill of Rights, that impressed me a lot. I found out the printing of the Bill of Rights was actually done by sympathetic English printers, it wasn't done in Southern Ireland at all it was done over here in London. Presumably they hadn't got any printing presses or it was too difficult politically.

The symposium lasted about four or five days, we had a good time, talked to each other, got to know each other, and then I went back to Barcelona for the last month. On my arrival there was a note 'where have you been' from my friend Nigel, the vicar from Lincolnshire, who had got his dates mixed up. I told him when to come over and when I was there but he came while I was in Dublin. I eventually found him living on the beach with some black men who had taken care of him. Pep had realised when I was coming back and got in touch with me, so I took Nigel to meet Pep and Nuri but they didn't get on at all. It ended up with Nigel getting very drunk and very aggressive and then he said 'come on we're going' and I said 'no I'm staying here, you can go, here's the door key go and let yourself in' and luckily he went back to England the day after, he didn't stay very long. Nigel had some severe problems but he was one of those people that you meet in life and you just can't help liking.

Pep and I used to do a lot of dancing, going to Plaza de Royal, and there was a place called Karma, I think it was in Gracia. These were disco places, and because I was English I got in, everyone else queued and Pep used to push me to the front and because I was English I got in. We all had some fun there and I met this young lady while dancing, her name was Suzanna, she was a hairdresser, *pellicuer.* One morning about 6 o'clock, somebody was banging on my door and it was her, she'd just turned up, so I started an affair with her. She was married, and I think she'd most probably had an affair with Pep as well at some time. She was a bit of a character but very nice, I was quite fond of her in a way but I didn't really make it a policy to have affairs with married women so I don't know why I got into that, partly I suppose because I knew it wasn't going to last, and it didn't much after that summer.

There were two things that happened that I was quite interested in because of the political overtones. I think it was that time that Sting had sung in Barcelona, the thing about Pinochet, and Pep had a recording of it. It was in Portuguese and Spanish and I tried to get hold of a copy but I've never been able to track it down. You can get hold of a couple of the tracks but you can't get the whole thing. And also of course when I was in Dublin I was listening to Irish music, Celtic music, which I also found quite interesting.

Pep had introduced me to Luis Luc. Luis Luc was a Catalan singer who sang some political songs when Franco was in power, because by the time I got there in the 1980s they'd only been rid of Franco for ten years or so. So it was that summer that Pep took me to Plaza de Neri. Plaza de Neri is a little plaza off the cathedral and I did a drawing of it, of some kids at the fountain.

It's a very small plaza, with buildings round two sides, depending which way you come into it. There's a sort of church-cum-school and also on the other side another building that houses the shoe museum of Barcelona, which is quite an interesting place. Problem is it never seemed to be open, but in the end I did get into it years later with my daughter.

But there were bullet holes all around the plaza, up to about human height, about 5 foot 6, so something nasty had taken place there. And there were only two entrances into the plaza, so if you came into the plaza and you've got somebody coming in both entrances, there was no way out. It was debatable who had got killed there, I said to Pep it was most probably Franco's men killing the republicans and he said, well maybe not, maybe it was Bolsheviks killing the Poum (the Workers' Party of Marxist Unification), or some of the other factions because there were a lot of different factions that Orwell describes, like the Anarchists, the UGT, the CNT. Anyway it's still got that awful resonance, all those bullet holes they've never bothered to cover up, partly because all the buildings around the little plaza are made of stone and of course when a bullet hits you've got a bullet hole but you've also got like a shattering around the hole. Very nasty stuff, and I began to get quite interested in the history of Barcelona and Pep was quite informative about that because he is quite a Catalan Anarchist. There were lots of trade unions that were there in the 1930s in the revolution which are still there now, so there was a lot of interest there for me, and a lot of it seemed to tie in with other things. I began to see things that had happened at the beginning of the century when Picasso was there, there were a lot of things that were happening politically I was thinking about, as well as artistically.

At that time there was a museum of modern art in the park Ciutadella and the National Gallery at the top of Plaça d'Espanya Montjuic and the Miro Foundation already there. I don't know when the Miro Foundation went up, it's quite a modern building. There wasn't the MACBA like there is now, but there were lots of museums and things to see, so I really did come back thinking 'I wish I lived out there' because it was quite a cultural experience, and of course politically there was a sort of wakening up for the Catalans. They'd been under heavy pressure during the Franco time so they got a bit crazy in a way. They'd gone a bit sex and drug mad, but at the same time there was a very earnest wanting to get themselves back to the position that they rightly owned, because they'd always been considered the second capital of Spain, and in the modern period the second capital of art after Paris. People went from there to Paris because there wasn't the big art scene in Barcelona that there was in Paris so Picasso and Casagemas and others left, even Ramon Cassas had visits to Paris.

I came back to Cambridge for the new academic year, but Pep and Nuri said 'just come back any time, just phone us up'. I started back teaching at the art school, I'd been to Ireland, and I was just thinking, well perhaps I ought to change my life in some way, and it was then that I started to think about exchanging with Mary at Sonoma State University.

But in the meantime I'd had the TUC exhibition, I was back to making art but mainly like I said before doing drawings. I just didn't have the time to be at the church, and not only that, I was on my own and it was quite an isolated place to be on your own. So when Pep and Nuri said I could come back, I became a regular visitor. I used to go about three times a year during the holidays. That was good for me because I stayed with them, it didn't cost me very much and I saw a lot of the coastline. I went to Sitges, where there is a really good museum in what was Rusinol's house. Rusinol was a friend of Picasso's, with Ramon Cassas. He was slightly older than Picasso, Picasso was only 15 or 16 at the time and Sitges later became the hub of the gay fraternity as well. In the meantime I had come across Amodovar's films, so there was a lot happening in Catalonia and Spain and it was just very interesting to see it. It was very interesting for me because at that time the industrial state of Barcelona was still there that had been there since the nineteenth century so it was a different place from what it is now. They had started to think about restoring things including the Gaudis, and Parc Güell, but it hadn't actually happened then, it started to happen when they got them ready for the 1992 Olympics.

So suddenly you'd got all this building work taking place and unfortunately one of the side-effects was to pull down a lot of the old 19th century artisan centres and that was a shame really. Once you got out of Barcelona, 10-15 minutes along the coast, you were still in Barcelona but it was very industrialised with small artisans' workshops and that's all gone now, the large new industry is on the periphery of Barcelona in Montaro and places like that, so the 19th century ones are not seen any more. But it was really a pity because there were some really interesting industrial brick buildings that have all been pulled down.

The Gaudis stayed, there were lots of new apartment blocks which were for the Olympic village and supposedly they were going to be handed over to the poor people of Barcelona which of course never happened. When I was at the Irish symposium as I said, I met the architects who were working on the changes in Barcelona in preparation for the 1992 Olympics. I think there were over five new parks they made, and a park consisted of a recreation ground, sometimes new children's play things, climbing frames etc, not swings and roundabouts, they were much more modern than that, and pieces of sculpture. Some of the sculptures were new pieces, others were resurrected pieces which they'd incorporated, and they put them on new bases and made it all part of the modern thing. Jose Claro was one of the most classical of sculptors there from well before that period, he was in the 1930s the 1940s. He was a student of Maillol the French sculptor and he did a lot of very beautiful women sitting down in marble and they're part of the decor of Barcelona. There was another sculptor, Josep Llimona, who's got a very nice piece in Cuitadella Park, but he was the beginning of the 20th century, late 19th century. So there were pieces of Tapies' sculpture, there were all sorts of different contemporary pieces, but at the same time there were traditional pieces too that they'd kept. It was a huge restoration programme and it was incredible because before that you couldn't really see the Gaudi mosaics for all the dirt and the dust, they were absolutely transformed after they restored them. They restored the ones in Passeig de Gracia, the ones in Parc Güell, they did a magnificent job to get them ready in time for the 1992 Olympics as well as do all the Olympic buildings and everything.

I never got to go to the Olympics, I'm not fanatically mad about sport. I generally watch the World Cup every four years and I do watch the Olympics on telly but I've never made a point of going, because of course if you're watching the runners or something they've gone past and that's all you see, while actually you see more of them on the television. So I've never quite understood the attraction, I suppose it's the atmosphere of going.

The next time I went out to Barcelona I met the architects and they showed me the plans and everything in their office, and the following time I went I met Ian Hunter, who was responsible for doing the MA in Barcelona for Winchester School of Art. I just happened to be down by the Picasso Museum and I'd seen this building with printing presses in it and I was quite interested to know what was going on. Just as I was hanging about outside trying to get a look, this chap came out, and I started talking to him and we went off to a café and had a drink. At that time he was quite interested in me applying for the job of looking after it, because the person who was doing it was only temporary, but it never came to anything.

Chapter 11 - Second Marriage 1989-94

I started going out to Barcelona on a regular basis and I was still teaching sculpture at Cambridge College of Art and Technology, which was to become part of Anglia Polytechnic University and, eventually, Anglia Ruskin University. I also taught life drawing on Friday to the print-making students. There were two big beautiful rooms full of light for life drawing at the top of the art school, and I became friendly with the lecturer who was teaching in the other room. He was a good painter, Adrian Ryan, of the same generation as Daphne Herrion, and was quite well known in the 1940s and 50s. He used to exhibit at the Redfern Gallery in London and he was quite a character. He was a completely different personality to me, he'd gone to Eton public school, but he and I got on. In fact he taught me a lot about drawing, not about the practicalities of drawing, but he knew a lot more about who had drawn and when and what drawings to look out for. He had been a friend of Lucien Freud and he knew Augustus John and had collected Gwen John's work. He and his first wife Peggy had lived in and been part of the Mousehole artists in the 1940s. He had a brother who was mad about horse racing and who unfortunately got into serious debt, and Adrian sold his collection and bailed him out, which would have been worth a lot of money these days, he had a lot of really good art. He had a very beautiful drawing by Gwen John which he managed to keep, and a lot of other things that he had picked up over time in the West End of London. When he was collecting in the 1930s and 40s you could get things quite reasonably if you'd come from that sort of public school background and you knew where to look, not the prices you'd have to pay nowadays. I found him a really interesting person, very entertaining, but a bit strange, very conservative, and a great Thatcher fan, we used to have so many arguments about that.

He'd managed to get hold of a Camden Arts studio, they were rented to artists, he probably got it just before the Second World War and then in the 1960s or 70s they decided to pull them down and build other artists' studios. There was a little block of them off Camden High Street and he got one of those and of course when Thatcher came in he managed to buy one. It was a beautiful little place, incredibly beautiful for the middle of London, and it was set back, you didn't even know they existed. It was very small, there was just a studio downstairs with a little terrace outside and a mezzanine floor that you slept on. He lived there with his third wife Sue, who at that time worked for Bodley Head, she used to chase the printers and make sure they got it all done properly. She used to come in to the Cambridge College of Art and lecture to the illustration and graphics students to tell them it's not just a question of doing the drawings, somebody's got to do the printing of them for the illustrations in books. They were a nice couple, she was my age and he was 24 years older than me, he was always telling me that he and I were both monkeys in the Chinese horoscope.

 He was a very good tutor, he'd get all the students together and give them a really good critique, and he was very temperate, he used to really bring out the best in the students. He was always saying to me how to bring out the best in life drawing from the students and I started doing a lot of life drawings myself, because I hadn't really done any since Croydon. I found myself teaching life drawing, and it wasn't difficult to teach, but it was better when I started to do a lot more myself. I used to go and visit him because he had that studio but he also had a house, one of his relatives had an estate at Holbrook in Suffolk and on the estate was a little brick house which he let Adrian use. So he was half the time in London and half the time in Holbrook, it was down near the estuary and it was really nice to go down there and see him. He had a little vegetable plot. He was working away at trying to exhibit and sell his paintings. I really like the oils that he did much earlier on in his life, some of his still lifes of fish were very beautiful. I was always hankering after one but I never got one, but he did give me three or four water colours which I've got and several of his drawings. He used to draw on the student's page in the corner, show them how it went, and he used to tear the pieces off and give them to me sometimes. I used to do the same thing, but I never used to tear them off, I wish I had done now.

Because I'd won these competitions when I was young which got me into art school, I was always enthusiastic about drawing, and early on, by the time that I was going to Zen Buddhism, I realised there was a connection between the book *Zen in the Art of Archery* and drawing, because it's a discipline, the same, and sometimes you have to take in a lot of information but at the same time you have to let go too. It's not just about getting the human being in proportion, it's about getting some character, and that's most important, to get the actual character of the person and then the expression, your expression, whatever sort of drawing you do. The great thing with Adrian was that he opened up my eyes to all the different sorts of drawings. We talked about the French painters, about Matisse's and Picasso's drawings, about Michelangelo's drawings and Delacroix, we talked about so many different forms of life drawing.

We talked ages about Picasso because Picasso was a huge figure to him as well as to me, and the way that Picasso treated women, I didn't always see that side of him he saw, I think he felt that you should appear that way as a man treating women but he didn't treat his women like that. His three wives, he didn't seem to treat them abominably at all, they were all very friendly. When he had an exhibition they all came, and all the children came. He had three daughters Viv, Scarlett and Geraldine, and Geraldine was the same age as his third wife, Sue.

He was a tremendous character and he did teach me a lot about the different ways people have of teaching. He wasn't like that very 1960s way of teaching which was 'I do this, this is the only way it can be done' he was a much broader person than that. I rather liked that, I suppose because that was different from when I was at St Martin's, when Caro was the dominant person and then Philip King. But the teaching at Croydon School of Art hadn't been like that, so I was used to being a lot more open about the ways in which people should do things, and not just stick to 'everybody has to do welded metal sculpture' or whatever.

We used to talk endlessly in the Six Bells at lunchtime, we always used to go for a drink at lunchtime and get a sandwich or something. Nearly always we were just on our own talking about art, sometimes other members of staff would be there but most of the time it was just us two. Then I used to see him and his wife sometimes in the holidays, if I wasn't in Barcelona, and he became very helpful too. There was a person who was looking after and selling his paintings called Julian Machin who he got to have a look at my sculpture, and Julian started to see if he could sell pieces for me. He got me an introduction to the Redfern, but Redfern weren't interested in the sort of work that I was doing. I was very very fond of Adrian and our friendship carried on right until he died of cancer, much much later.

About that time a young lady came to be my model and she'd got her little girl with her, a very young baby. She modelled for me for about nine months, and by that time the baby was about 18 months. I didn't think much of her at all at the time; I was seeing an ex-art student who was a watercolour artist who lived in Cambridge. It wasn't an affair, we were just seeing each other. I was looking after Daphne's house at that time and she used to come round to Daphne's. I didn't really think much about it but when it came to St Valentine's Day I got a card through my letterbox, a very beautiful hand painted watercolour, and so naturally I thought it was this girl.

When I was teaching life drawing on the Friday, one of the girl students said to me 'did you get any Valentine's cards?', typical girl of 18 or 19, so I said, yes I got a really nice watercolour, and this girl said well do you know who it was from, and I said yes, I think I do, I think it was this watercolour artist who I've been seeing.

Anyway after the session Jo the model came up to me and she said 'It wasn't her, it was me' and stomped off and that's how I got to know my second wife! So we started off on a bad footing, I should have realised then.

She was living in a women's refuge when she first started modelling for me. She then got a council flat because she said her first husband was violent and was threatening her and the little girl. I didn't question it very deeply, I think sometimes you go along with things because you want to go along with them

Angie's not my biological daughter, and she's never seen her biological father because Jo said he was violent. I've never adopted her because Jo refused to let me adopt her and I should have realised then that the relationship wasn't as sound as I thought it was.

We started to see each other and I suppose within about four or five months we'd started living together. I'd already built the mezzanine floor at the church, to sleep on, and we put a cot up there for Angie. Adrian was quite pleased about that because he actually liked Jo but he also liked Angie, he was very very fond of children, especially little girls, as he had three daughters of his own, they were big girls then.

It was like a different period for me because suddenly I'd got somebody where before I was on my own. Jo had done A-level Spanish, so she could speak Spanish really well, and she started coming out to Barcelona and meeting Pep and Nuri and they all got on. Then Pep and Nuri started to have one or two holidays with us in Scotland, because I felt I should pay them back, they were always putting us up. They didn't want to come to England very much but they did come to Scotland even though as you know, Scotland isn't always the warmest even in the middle of summer.

I realised that Jo had sort of done a nosedive, there she was in a women's refuge, and she needed some support and help. I was much older of course. She started painting on silk, and I encouraged this, and she started having a stall on the craft market in Cambridge, where she would sell things. Then we had one productive time when Nuri said 'I've got a friend who's got a shop in Barcelona, if you bring over some of your silks she might buy them' and she bought them straight off Jo. But I don't think Jo was really interested in carrying on and making a business out of it, so it never went any further. It was a shame because it did have a possibility, but then at that time she hadn't got a degree or anything.

We started talking about her going back to art school, and she obviously didn't want to be in the same place I was teaching at, so that was a problem. My problem was doing my work as usual and trying to bring up a young daughter, which was strange in a way because we didn't start off too well, me and Angie. I remember the first outing I took Jo and Angie to, it was Clumber Park which is up the A1 just a bit further on than Sherwood Forest. It's a very nice park, it's got lots of old trees, it was very beautiful and we found a restaurant there and Angie was throwing bits of food and making a mess of the place. When we put the cot up on the mezzanine floor I got these really lovely post cards of animals, ducks and tigers and all sorts of animals, and put them all up around the cot and she used to just stand up and pull them off the wall. As soon as I'd put them back she would pull them off, and this was some kind of winding-Douglas-up game, but she was 2 by then and it was the terrible twos. My son wasn't too bad at 2, he wasn't like that, but Angie was pretty awful, in a playful way.

We settled into a pattern where I was really nice to her from then on. I suppose the relationship didn't really start to gel until she started going to nursery school. Jo nearly always picked her up, but sometimes I picked her up, and then when she started to go to school I started taking a real interest. At that time Jo had got the craft market so she was working on Saturdays, so I could take Angie and one or two of her friends out to different places and we used to have a really good time.

There was one particular time, around Christmas, when I took them to a little dance theatre place in Cambridge called Covent Garden Dance, and there was an extraordinary man there. He was a one-man band and he'd got all these boxes and different puppets, aeroplanes etc. When you went in there you sat down in a Bedouin tent, I suppose there were only enough seats for about 15 people. The show was *The Travels of Munchhausen,* and everything was puppets and open boxes and then there were First World War planes that came over by pulling strings. It was phenomenal and I don't know what happened to the man but I talked to him afterwards, he was Italian and he'd just finished art school in Italy. It was absolutely incredible, the kids were quiet for the whole hour there. I was mesmerised and all the kids were mesmerised. He'd got these little boxes and one box was like an aquarium and stuff and he'd got everything going on but we all sat in this Bedouin tent and it was absolutely gorgeous.

So we had time together, quality time, and then I got into reading to her which I'd done with my son. I got into reading the classics like *Wind in the Willows* and *Winnie the Pooh* and all the rest of them because they were things that I'd enjoyed and I think that gives a child a sense of belonging, especially things like *Wind in the Willows*, the sense of a real belonging and understanding of different places, especially if you live in a city, because otherwise children don't realise what the countryside is like. The whole opening of spring and dusting the cobwebs and Ratty and Mole by the riverside, all that I think is so important and I suppose then our relationship started to take on quite a deep meaning, even a bit deeper than with my son in some ways, I think my son and I had a different sort of way of expressing our fondness for each other.

It was about then that I began to have my first doubts about the relationship with Jo. I didn't want the relationship to end because suddenly I'd got this daughter who used to sit on the windowsill at the flat in Cambridge to wait for me to come home, I mean only a little girl could do that, a boy wouldn't do it, sit on the windowsill looking out the window waiting for me.

One of her friends was a little girl called Shirley. Her parents came from mainland China, he was a PhD student studying economics at Cambridge University, Shu-Fa, and we got on, Jo and I and Shu-Fa and Wa, Shirley's mother. Wa was incredibly beautiful and she was also intelligent, she'd studied warfare at University in China, she was a strategist I believe, which seemed a bit strange, I never quite understood it. I started taking Shirley out with Angie on Saturdays, and Shirley was really weird because she was always throwing her arms around me. In fact Angie used to get quite jealous sometimes because she was very physically orientated towards me.

Wa said to me 'I think you ought to teach Shirley drawing. We can't afford to pay you but we'll teach you calligraphy' so I thought 'well that sounds nice' but she really was extremely beautiful, in the Chinese sort of way, she was the same age as Jo, and even then I thought, 'this is going to be dangerous'.

But I agreed, and I used to go round there and teach Shirley drawing and Shu-fa was never there and Wa used to teach me calligraphy. We got closer and closer, and I started writing her poetry, not writing it myself, I started finding it for her, because I'd always been interested in poetry, and when I was studying Zen I got interested in Japanese, Chinese and Korean poetry, so I'd got a lot of books on it.

It came to the sports day for Angie and Shirley at their little school, and Wa was there, and I came with Jo and I just thought, this is no good. Jo saw me look at her and I just thought, 'I've got to tell her about it', so I told her about it and she said 'well, she does make passes at you, it's not just you' but she wasn't worried. The amazing thing with Jo was that she wasn't worried, but it was a sort of staging post for me, because once I'd told her I didn't feel anything any more. I still found Wa beautiful, but once I'd told Jo I didn't feel that anything was going to happen. I'd made a decision, it's like giving up smoking, you make a decision and you stick to it.

After I'd told Jo about Wa, about two days later, Wa and Shu-Fa arrived at the door. And Wa said to me, he was supposed to go back to Beijing, but he wouldn't go back because she'd talked to him about me and he felt insecure, but as far as I know they're still together.

Then I decided perhaps it would be a good thing to get away somewhere, and so I wrote off for this Fulbright Scholarship. I didn't think I would get it, but I did, to do sculpture and lectures on public art. They wrote back to me and asked whether I had got anybody to exchange with, so I contacted Mary, the sculptor I'd met at the Irish public art symposium and she said 'I'd love to come but can you arrange for my daughter to come free to the University?', Anglia Polytechnic University, which the old Cambridge College of Art and Technology had become by then. So I said to Jo 'well if you want to come with me', because I hadn't asked her, 'if you want to go to the art school, perhaps we can arrange for Mary's daughter to exchange with you'. We agreed that, and it would be much easier if we were married so I said to Jo 'do you want to marry me?' and her face just lit up. I'll never forget that, it just lit up and I was quite shocked at that, because she wasn't one to show a lot of emotion. Funny what relationships you get yourself into, isn't it? So, we got married and we had a really nice wedding day and we were set to go to America.

Chapter 12 - California 1994-95

In 1994 we went to California and the idea was that Jo did her first year at the university in exchange for Mary's daughter doing creative writing at Anglia Polytechnic University, as CCAT had become by then, and Mary exchanged with me. And that worked very well, but there was a problem because the exchange was full time and I was only a fractional appointment. I went to the head of the art school over there and said, 'I'm not doing five days a week because I'm not paid for it', but they were okay about that, and also I was entitled to research for the money that the Fulbright Scholarship had given me for writing up papers on public sculpture.

I'd been planning to visit Albert Elsen, who was the big authority on Rodin, because I met him at the symposium on public sculpture in Dublin in 1988 and he'd invited me over. Unfortunately he'd died the year before, but I still went to Stanford University and saw his collection, it was quite a nice collection of Rodin. I made a tour of the other universities in the area as well, I went to Berkeley and also to Mills College to listen to a talk there and participate in the discussion. I also went to some smaller art schools in the Bay Area, to give talks and things. It was a really informative time.

We were well looked after, there were I think 200 or 300 Fulbright scholars from all over the world in the Bay Area in California in the same year that I was there. I was the only artist, most of the others were seismologists so we made friends with quite a few seismologists, one from Turkey I remember, there was another one from Greece and one in particular a nice lady who came from Beijing University who invited us out to Beijing, but unfortunately we never got there. It was interesting to listen to what they were doing there and it was quite exciting actually living on the fault line. They seemed to have built all the new universities, the new housing estates the new schools along the fault line which is actually disastrous as they explained to me. If they do have another major quake like they had in 1906, what will happen with California is that because the fault line runs some way along the river bed, when it shakes the sandy soil will mix with the water and then just suck everything into it. The Turkish guy told me how this had happened in 1985 in Turkey where a whole village had disappeared into the mud, it just sucks it all down. So they have been rather silly building things along the fault line. The most expensive places in California are on the bedrock, as they call it, because they're more stable. The 1906 quake seems to have gone for San Francisco more than other parts, but then there wasn't the building along the fault-line in those days, they had built on the bedrock.

We got taken out about six times during the year to meet the other Fulbright scholars in a social gathering. We spent a rainy day on the coast trying to look at elephant seals on duck-boards. It was so muddy we had to walk along these duck-boards and you could only see them from a distance because it was absolutely pelting down with rain. There were these huge fat lumps in the distance. There were various other excursions, I can't remember what they all were now. We got taken to a Pueblo village which I thought looked like a stage set, I didn't really like it. It was part of Mexico before the American-Mexican war, the whole of Arizona and California was part of Mexico, so there is still that influence and there are a lot of Mexicans there.

We had a big gathering of 200 of us in an enormous Chinese restaurant in San Francisco for a Christmas party. It was really exciting because the Fulbright scholars had got their children with them, so Angie loved it because there were other kids there, who couldn't always speak English but nevertheless they seemed to all get on very well. Most of the Fulbright scholars from across the world did speak English, not all of them, but some were better than others.

Angie and her mum went ice skating at a big ice skating rink in San Francisco. It was Angie's first time and she really enjoyed it. I didn't do it, I was too much of a coward. I had gone ice skating when I was a kid, my cousin Jackie used to take me ice skating in Streatham, London, the one who went to art school before me, but I didn't fancy it when I was out there.

It was an exciting time. We saw lots of exhibitions of course, and we went to visit museums and art works. I was particularly impressed by the Diego Rivera mural in the Art Institute in San Francisco. There were other things I wasn't so impressed by. I wasn't too impressed by the Richard Serra which was outside a very old building, I'm not quite sure if the two things went together scale-wise but there was a lot to see.

And of course I was making sculpture and it started to reflect the place I was in. I made a piece called *Buttress* which looks as if it's holding up a building, that sort of buttress shape. I remember when I was a child going to visit my great-grandmother, the one who looked like a witch, her house was buttressed up, because it had started to come apart, presumably during the bombing in the war. I remember these huge pieces of wood holding up the building and I was quite interested in portraying some idea of the place so I made that. And I made a couple of other sculptures that were I suppose to do with the light, they were continuing on the sort of lattice work I'd made in the 1980s.

Sonoma was a big university in its own grounds, it had its own botanical gardens which Angie and I used to visit quite a lot in the summer, because it was nice to have our lunch outside. One day we were sitting outside having our lunch and there was this huge thud, literally about a foot away from us, and it was a cone the size of a football, it actually came from a monkey puzzle tree and if it had landed on us it would have done us some damage because it was very, very heavy and I took it back to the flat and kept it.

The art department was in a very funny place, it was like a western fort, with a high wooden fence around it and big double gates. When you went in the gate, on the left hand side was the bronze foundry, on the right hand side there was a huge metal-working shop and then next door to that there was a wood-working shop with incredible machines that I've never seen over here.

Opposite that was the ceramics department with huge kilns that they used for making rather large vases and pots and ceramic sculpture. So it was quite an interesting place, and then beyond that was the interior of the art school where print making and fine art went on.

There were lots of restrictions. They had a lot of facilities in the sculpture department but not really geared to the sort of work I was doing in plastic. It was more designed for heavy metal, Anthony Caro, David Smith sort of stuff, or bronze casting, it didn't have things for cutting and bending plastic. So I had to try and get all that and do it in the garage where we were living. The students had never done any stone carving, and they were crying out for me to teach it, so I got to know a place in San Francisco called Renaissance Stone where they sold stone for sculptors. He was a really interesting guy and very helpful and I bought some stone for myself because I couldn't resist it, once I'd gone in to buy some for the students and seen all this stone. Mostly it was alabaster and soapstone but very different from the alabaster and soapstone we get here back in Europe. So I was making lots of different things, I was making these lattice-type things and also some things out of cardboard and some stonework because a lot of the time I couldn't get any acrylic sheet.

There were a number of things that I did with the students which were projects. They'd never done any environmental sculpture and they were eager to do some bronze casting. I was quite interested in teaching them stone carving and bronze casting and it was good for me because I'd taught stone carving back in England but I hadn't taught bronze casting. It was interesting to work alongside the students because when you're bronze casting, it's a team effort, you can't do it on your own, you have to have responsible students who are going to help you because you've got to have at least two people to pour the bronze, you've got to have other people to take off the dross, so you've got to have a really good team, about six or seven people altogether.

Bronze casting is rather a big technical thing to do and there were about ten students who were interested in doing something and of course I was interested in doing it myself. To cut the process down a bit, you can make the figure directly out of wax, instead of clay which you then have to cast in wax, and then you heat up the wax and the wax comes out and then you pour in the bronze, although it's not quite as simple as that. I gave them the option of either doing that or making it straight in wax, but if you make it straight in wax it's got to be quite thin so normally what they do with a classical piece of bronze sculpture is they make the wax hollow and they put what they call 'investment' inside which is either a mixture of plaster and grog or plaster and sand and they hold it in place through the wax model with nails then put investment very thickly on the outside. What we had to do was actually suspend the wax model in a big tub - if the model was only about a foot high you would have to suspend it in something that was about 3ft deep in the middle and about 18in wide because when you pour in the bronze it's got to take the shock of the bronze going into the investment. If you didn't do that, if it was thinner, the investment would crack open. So it's quite a lengthy process to make your wax, to put the investment inside the wax, and the wax is quite thin, inside, you've got this figure like a skin of the figure that you've made in wax, you've got investment inside the wax and you've got this big investment outside.

The American system was slightly different because in England we don't have such a big investment because we bury it in the sand, we have a big sand pit and pummel and squash the sand down with a pummeler so that the investment can't break open with the shock of the bronze. But in America all they did was put huge amounts of investment on, tie it round with wire and then just lay it on the sand when you pour the bronze, because obviously if the bronze spills over it won't move on sand, whereas if it was tiles or something it would move. They had a new method which has come in now called ceramic shell, but the problem is they had all the stuff there for ceramic shell, but at that time they hadn't really got it to work properly, because you need to dip the wax in this ceramic shell and leave it for so many seconds and dip it again and somebody hadn't worked it out, so I thought it was best to do it the conventional way with investment.

Then you wheel these huge investment pieces which are like a lump of stone, they're 3ft high and 18in-2ft wide, you wheel them into walk-in kilns, and you have to turn them upside down, and they're quite heavy, you turn them upside down, wheel them into a walk-in kiln, and that dries out the investment because you can't have any water in the investment when you pour the bronze, because it shoots the bronze out from the investment and also it drains out all the wax, leaving your figure inside, the skin of your figure, as it were. And then while the investment is still warm, you've already gone into the foundry, bumped up your furnaces to get your bronze hot in big crucibles, you've put in the oxidiser into the bronze, and for that foundry, because it could do fairly big 1ft, 2ft bronzes, we had an overall gantry which moved the crucibles over to the investment and all we had to do was actually tilt it and pour it, which is still an art in itself, because you've got to make sure that you don't get covered in it. So we had to move them fairly quickly from the walk-in kilns, which were in the ceramic department, through into the foundry, on a hot summer's day, put them in the sand and then we had to dress ourselves in special boots, special trousers, all leather, a leather coat, a leather apron and a helmet and a visor, and gloves of course. Then you go and get the bronze out and pour it into the investment, then you leave it to cool down. We left it for a day or so and then you have to chip all the investment away, it comes away fairly easily but you've got your runners and risers. The runners and risers have been added onto the wax figure, they're just wax rods that make sure the bronze goes to every part of the figure but also takes the air away because if you just poured in the bronze the air would still be there and it would be trapped, so you've got what they call risers to take the air away, so you have to cut those off because you don't want those on your figure.

And then, they sandblasted it, I didn't like that, because it did leave the surface a little pitted, I thought it was a bad idea to do after we'd done it, I'd never sandblasted it before, it was the Americans doing things quickly rather than using just a wire brush and cleaning it all up. You file down where the runners and risers are and you clean it up and then you've got the option of what patina to put on the bronze, whether you want it green or you want it black or you want it still bronzey coloured, so that's another process in itself which I got the students to do, either cold or hot patinas. Then you've got your finished bronze and you've got to mount them on some sort of base.

So, a lengthy procedure which took a month or so to do, I suppose, all the different stages and explaining the procedure to the students. One of the students, Andreas, who was of Mexican origin, helped me because some of the processes they used over there were different, like not burying the bronze, we'd always buried the investment, and he said, no, we just leave it on top, so he was very helpful, and I'm still in touch with him, he lives in south California. It's quite interesting seeing the photographs, because I am the smallest person in the room, the others are all six foot odd! And we had a great time doing this and after we'd done it, we celebrated - they have really good beers in California, they had a beer with chilli in it which I loved.

The other thing that we did was go to the Russian Gulch to do an environmental piece. I said 'well, first of all we'll go off to this bay and you should think about it' and we took all sorts of different materials, but the main thing was to make a sculpture and an environmental piece, more of an installation piece, while we were there, which some of them did. It was a rather nice occasion because it was a weekend so I took my daughter and my wife and Angie helped. We made something out of hessian. I've actually got a film of it but of course it's an American VHS or the equivalent, I'm thinking about trying to get it converted but I'm not sure if I'm looking forward to seeing it because some of the things with the American students worked out well, and with others, sometimes they just didn't get the plot. They weren't really very up on environmental things and on installations and happenings, funnily enough, at Sonoma, and yet there were a lot of happenings in the 1960s and 70s in California but it doesn't seem to have reached that part or it had been forgotten.

I wasn't too happy with the cold, it does get cold out there. It's very strange, very beautiful light, it's sort of green and red, sort of shadows, very much like the light you get in the Costa del Luz in Spain, I suppose because it's also on the south western coast. And I really enjoyed the Diego Riveras like I said, I got quite interested in trying to see as much of his work as I could, and started reading up about it.

We went to Santa Barbara while we were there, to the museum of Santa Barbara where there was an English sculptor, Andy Goldsworthy, having an exhibition, and we drove all the way down past the Big Sur, down to where Clint Eastwood was the Mayor of Carmel. Carmel was a very strange place, we'd actually stayed in a hotel not far away and drove there in the morning. We parked the car and the first impression of Carmel, it was like the house in Snow White and the Seven Dwarves, they were pretty little houses, but they were all small, they were another scale, they weren't a proper American scale, they were all smaller. I found out later that it was built as an artists' community, but then of course, what happens with artists' communities, the rich come in and buy them up. It was a very strange place, street after street of these little wooden places. We got down on the beach and all the people we saw there was something wrong with them. I kept looking at my wife and she kept looking at me, and thinking, what is it that's strange about these people, and then we realised that, because they'd got so much money, they'd had face-lifts, so they were old people looking young, and they walked like a young person, because they'd obviously spent money on their joints and god knows what but it was really weird! It was a very weird sensation.

There were many things in America that I felt uncomfortable about. When I was teaching the students, they didn't have any sense of Europe, where Europe was, where England was. One or two had been to Europe but most of them hadn't. They didn't know where London was; one of them thought Paris was the capital of Europe. They didn't have any sort of idea because of course they come from a place where states have their own autonomy but Washington is the capital, so they thought that Paris was the capital of Europe. They didn't really understand that Europe is not a single country like the USA. There was a lot of stuff they just couldn't get it into their heads at all, that sort of difference in the way of life between the English and the French and the Italians and of course the Americans. So it was quite difficult in that way, I found them kind of provincial, I found the whole of California very closed-minded.

Obviously California had gone through different times, in the 1960s, in the hippy times, it was the place to be, there was a lot of interesting stuff going on, and then of course when Silicone Valley happened. But sometimes you get this blossoming, but then you get the opposite, the sort of redneck reaction, so when we were there it was gradually becoming more right wing. They'd done away with their state radio, they had to have this sponsorship to keep the state radio going. There was still City Limits and we went to see the bookshop where Ferlinghetti did the publishing and I bought some books there, really good books. There were some remnants of the sort of California I'd heard about, but it was a changed place, I felt it was much more right-wing than I'd been expecting. I have memories about California but they're very different, in a way, from what I felt about Mexico. Mexico's in Central America and it's not far away but it's such a different attitude from the US.

I enjoyed teaching the students, a lot of the students were very nice and I really enjoyed meeting them and teaching them. We went to Washington

DC with the students, that was a good trip because we saw the Lincoln memorial and the Hirshhorn Museum, which has quite a lot of sculpture. I saw the Holocaust Museum and when you go into the Holocaust Museum they give you an identity of someone who was in the concentration camps, so you're actually walking around with their identity card and of course you don't know what's going to happen, although mine, the person I was, actually did survive. It's built so that as you walk around you get this feeling all the time of being channelled through, just like they were. It is a very good museum but it's awful to experience it.

There was a lot of interest for me in America because you've got these two different sides to America, you've got this left wing Democratic party and then you've got the Republicans on the right wing and it's there for you to see. One of the main things was going to the Vietnam memorial wall which is made of blocks of black granite stone with people's names on. The woman who did it, Maya Lin, at the time she won that competition for the Vietnam war memorial she was only a student, she was a student of architecture, and it is a fantastic piece of work. What I didn't realise until I was there was that people had used it, the gaps between, obviously they couldn't get marble as big as the corner type shape that it is, so each block is the same size with the same lettering with different names on and you've got a gap between them and people stuffed mementoes of their loved ones in these gaps. It appears that there's another museum in Washington because every now and again they have to clear them all away, and there's another museum, so I heard, with all these mementoes in that people put there.

But as soon as it was put up there was an outcry because they thought this was far too abstract so they asked for a three figure composition of soldiers so actually by that Vietnam War memorial you've got another memorial with these figurative pieces, these three soldiers. As soon as that was put up there was an outcry that of course there were women in the forces in Vietnam and so you got another three figure composition somewhere there of three nurses or three women doing something, which I saw as well, but of course nobody looks at them, people go down just to study these names, it is a very effective war memorial I think, really incredible work.

There were lots of things in Washington that impressed me, although the students didn't want to come, the students didn't come and see the

Vietnam War memorial with me and only a couple of them came to the Holocaust Museum. Most of them couldn't be bothered, which seemed very strange. A lot of the students have to earn their own living, and there was one particular student called Julie Montgomery, who seemed to be very set up with a house and a car for her age, she was only 19-20 a very good looking girl in a very magazine sort of way. When we eventually left America, came back, and I started working back at Cambridge in September, facing me was Julie Montgomery who'd come and registered herself, she was so impressed with my teaching she wanted to be taught for another year, and she stayed there for another year at Anglia. She could do that because, I didn't realise it at the time, but I found out she used to model for Vogue or one of those big magazines and this is how she got all her money, she had that sort of photogenic features and she really did work hard at it. She was a very nice girl and became quite a friend of the family - she was incredible actually because she wasn't bitchy, she wasn't spoilt, and I think it was because she'd earned this money herself. She stayed in Europe, she obviously worked while she was out here doing the modelling bit, but it gave her the money to be flexible and she was a lovely girl. She was very much into chance, the John Cage thing and also the I Ching and things like that. in fact she gave me a little present which I still have, a set of little cards that she made herself, you take one at random and read what it says.

We had some really good times while we were over there. Restaurants were very cheap in California, you could easily get a full meal for about £5 in those days, a three course meal with beer or whatever you wanted. There was a particular Vietnamese restaurant that was very good, run by a family that had come over after the Vietnam War, the man and his wife and daughter were very lovely, and there was a Thai restaurant too that was very good. It was cheap food and it was good food too. Also there was a lot of Mexican food, there was Mexican food on the campus, they allowed trailer things on the campus, because it had its own beautiful gardens and it was in its own grounds. It was very nice, but at the same time in some ways it was very provincial and we had some very strange encounters.

I had two technicians, Victor Crispin and John Scott. Vic was a huge man, almost 6ft6in and broad with it. He was born in Chicago, but his family had come from Norway originally, and he became a good friend. John Scott was okay, but he was a bit strange sometimes. I remember him inviting me to a stag night, it was all these divorced men who'd been married and they had a dinner together, and that was very nice because we went to this sushi restaurant which was lovely and very cheap. Another time I wasn't so pleased with him. It was when we went down to get the Renaissance stone I told you about for the students. He said 'I'll take you somewhere' and he took me to this grotty back street in San Francisco and all I remember is going in this metal door and in front of us there were loads of men drinking, and then he started paying dollars to see a woman dancing around a pole. That wasn't so bad in itself, he was just showing me what blokes get up to, but the woman was one of my students. It was a way for students to earn money. Luckily she was behind glass and couldn't see us, but I didn't think he should have taken me there and shown me.

The only really nasty time I had in California was when he and I were walking down San Francisco, and I heard somebody shouting across the street. I didn't know it was directed at us at all, I heard somebody shouting, I was in my forties, I wasn't stupid, I knew not to look, so we kept on walking. Suddenly John, who was behind me, just took off, he started running full pelt away from me and this bloke came over and started shouting almost in my face 'Fucking this and fucking that'. I just thought, just keep walking, don't speed up, don't slow down, just keep walking, and he still continued but he was behind me. I'll never forget it because I thought 'any minute I'm gonna get a knife in the back' because he was so aggressive, but in the end he gave up and I just kept walking. I got round the corner of this block and I said 'thank you John', no help from him at all and he said 'well, I'm not gonna get murdered'. That's what they're like, they're very strange, they've got this paranoia, because the man was obviously very violent but I don't know whether he would have actually done anything.

I remember another occasion, going out with John in San Francisco, and there was a bloke indicating left in front of me, so I flashed at him, and he said 'what did you do that for?' and I said 'well what should I have done?' and he said 'don't do that'. Because at that time there was a gang going round Los Angeles, and they had their indicator going, and every time somebody flashed them, they shot them. And I thought, this is ridiculous.

I'll never forget, another time when we got invited to a lecturer's house, he was giving a little party for all the lecturers and their wives, and we were invited. Suddenly we got onto the gun culture and I said, 'well of course, you lecturers don't have guns at home' and it all went quiet because they're no different from anybody else out there, they're paranoiac about somebody breaking in and killing them, and when you look at it it's not that bad. I mean there are quite a lot of murders in America but it's not that ridiculous, there are probably more murders in Mexico than there are in the United States.

Chapter 13 - Mexico 1995

While we were at Sonoma, we had the opportunity of taking the students to Mexico because it had been arranged to take some fine art students who wanted to do print-making to a little print-making art school in a place called Zacatecas. Now Zacatecas was a very very beautiful old colonial Spanish Mexican town, it's got a wonderful church and two big mask museums which are run by two brothers who also run the print-making studios. So we got some expert information there, and I think there was a bit of competition between the two brothers, Alejandro and Fernando, but they were really lovely to us and we enjoyed our stay.

The first thing that happened was we had problems with Angie at the customs because on her passport was the name that was on her birth certificate, her biological father's name, and of course it was different from my name although I was married to her mother by then. There was a problem on the Mexican side because there was a lot of pressure from the Americans about people who had had unhappy divorces trying to take American children out of the country through Mexico, and they were suspicious that this might be what was happening. We got the other art teacher, one of the print-making lecturers, Shane Weir, to speak up for us. Shane was a good friend, he went to the Royal College and had come from England in the sixties and married an American girl. He spoke up for us but it didn't make any difference, they wanted something in writing from Angie's biological father. So here we were stuck with all the students on the other side of the barricade, if you like, and I didn't know what to do. I just started to take some notes out of my pockets, pesos, and one of the men who was resisting us going through said 'just go away and write a letter'. I can't remember if it was me or Jo who went to the toilets, wrote a letter supposedly in Angie's biological father's name, gave it to the man with some money and then he stamped it and off we went.

So that was the start of quite an interesting journey, because on that journey we had to get a coach and Angie got locked in the toilet. She was about six or seven, she's locked in the toilet and she starts screaming. Now you don't know what's happening in the toilet, you are in the coach and you don't know what's happening to your daughter, who's screaming her head off, you don't know if there's a man in there with her, you don't know if there's some sort of animal in there, you don't know what's in there. The driver wouldn't stop, and we all had a go at him. In the end I think it was Shane who said: 'if you don't stop we're just going to open the door and you can take the consequences' so he stopped. My view of Mexicans is that generally they were very nice but this one wasn't. He'd obviously had this problem before because all he did was come to the back of the coach and lift the door off the hinges, he knew exactly how to do it so clearly it must have happened before and it wasn't her fault. Of course she was traumatised, just because she couldn't get out, it wasn't because there was anything in there, but we didn't know that at the time. We didn't know what was wrong with her, so that wasn't a very nice experience.

Then we found ourselves in a hotel in Guadalajara. Guadalajara is the sort of – well, it's got the nickname the shithole of Mexico. This accommodation which Shane had booked was a converted prison, there were downstairs cells and upstairs cells, which would have been where the guards used to walk around, because there were about twenty five, thirty students and about four members of staff: me, Shane and Victor who was the technician.

We were given the room next door to the toilets. We didn't think anything of it, the toilets didn't smell but as soon as we turned off the lights we could hear all these weird noises and thought what's that, and then suddenly my wife started screaming. The lights went on and there were cockroaches everywhere, because of course cockroaches like the damp and smelly parts. So then we had to create a stink there and get ourselves moved, to another cell upstairs, which was better.

The rest of the journey went okay and eventually we ended up in a really nice old colonial hotel in Zacatecas. But then there were difficulties there, because the farmers were on strike and they'd blockaded the road, they had brought all their Ford tractors into the main plaza, the square, of this old colonial town. That was quite unnerving because they weren't in a good mood. They had a legitimate grievance because they'd bought these tractors from the Ford Motor Company in America at a certain interest and then the banks had put the interest up so they went on strike. It was quite interesting because they called themselves Zapatistas, I didn't realise that Emil Zapata is still a big figure over there, they're still very left wing, and I was quite drawn to what was going on. Nobody else wanted to find out really, all the American people didn't want to know, they just wanted to avoid it. So I went to the square and started drawing these Zapatistas and then they started sharing their lunch with me, and they became more friendly to me, but they weren't very friendly to the American students, they kept calling them gringos but me, once they found out I was English, and my family was English, they were very nice to us. But they didn't want the Americans there and obviously there was a little bit of a problem there between the workers' politics and the tourist/cultural side of Zacatecas, because it is quite an artists' colony.

Alejandro was a really good sculptor, he did very fragile little things, which I really liked, beautiful little things made out of paper and wire and stuff, which he showed in Paris. I don't know if he showed them at home, I think most probably his outlet was in Paris. He and his brother Fernando ran the print-making school, so we went there to watch what they were doing. It was a really good set-up with presses and things, I think the students enjoyed themselves and it was a lovely little town to be in.

We were so enthralled that when we got back to Sonoma I said to Jo 'we must go back to Mexico' because it really is a place to see. Someone had told me before we left England that if I stayed out there for 366 days I wouldn't have to pay tax to the English government or the American government. I'd only got a visa for 365 days, but it was in my interest to stay there 366 days, we were booked to come out on the 365th day, but it was cheaper for me to get another flight for a day later and for my wife and my daughter to leave the day before. That wasn't until about the September, so when we'd finished the academic year, in May, we had three months until we were due to go back, so we went back to Mexico. The idea was to go to Mexico City to have a look at the mural painters, Orozco, Siqueiros and Diego Rivera, and Frida Kahlo's work, to have a look at the pyramids and then go on to Oaxaca.

Well we'd gone out to Mexico City and we booked in at this rather nice hotel. I was quite shocked, I found Mexico City was quite incredible, because it was a modern hotel, but from outside our bedroom window you could see an apartment block which had lost a wall in the 1985 earthquake. One wall had come away completely from this apartment block and people were still living in the apartments so you could see into their homes. There was still lots of dereliction from this earthquake, and this was 1994. In Mexico City you were very aware of the rich and the poor, it really did hit me for the first time, more than Zacatecas, because in Zacatecas you didn't really see so much difference in people's lives, but, it was the first time I think that it really hit me what a third world country was like. This was a huge city, it was quite unbearable in the summer, when we were there, the pollution took your breath away.

There were hundreds of mosquitoes and my wife had a phobia about mosquitoes. We'd become the centre of attraction for a small amount of time unbeknown to us. We had louvre windows in the hotel, you could close them but there were gaps, so my wife took to stuffing her bras and undies and my underpants and our daughter's undies and things into the gaps in the louvre windows to stop the mosquitoes. Well of course it could be seen from down in the street. So this became a joke, they kept laughing at us and we didn't really know what they were laughing about, but we did find out later.

Then I made a very stupid mistake. Taxis are very cheap out there, or they were for us. They have all these little beetle cars and what they do is take out the front passenger seat, that's where you put your suitcases, and you've only got the seats that can hold three people, in the back. So we were going all over the place by taxi. The underground was one peso and I thought it would be fun to go on it. We were in one of the ruins in Mexico City one day, the ruin of a temple, when a man started talking to us in English. He seemed to be well dressed, he asked us if we'd seen the archaeology museum, and he said 'tomorrow, if you take this metro line down to the archaeology museum I'll meet you there at ten o'clock'.

Well, I think he set us up to go on the underground, because we could have taken a taxi, but we decided to go and I think they were waiting for us, like they do in Barcelona, they actually wait for the tourists. They're very clever, they work out who's a tourist and then wait for them. As soon as we got on the train there was a woman who was talking to Angie. Now she was obviously Mexican but she could speak English, and she started talking to Angie so all our attention went to Angie. Like a stupid fool I'd got my passport on me, luckily I hadn't got Angie's and Jo's, I'd got money, and I'd got my camera in a little black bag, I've still got the bag.

It was quite a crowded train and there was a woman sitting down obviously trying to get my attention, she wasn't part of these people, I think she was just trying to warn us. There was a big man who kept standing in my way, I kept thinking, 'you've got the whole train, why do you keep standing in front of me?' a great big bloke, six foot something, huge man, and he didn't seem to have anything to do with this woman. Then there was this rather shifty character who was standing next to me but I didn't really take much notice at the time.

We had to change trains and as soon as I'd got out I knew by the weight of the bag that the camera had gone, and when I looked at the bag the straps were undone. The shifty man must have undone those straps while my attention was distracted. This is the way they work, there are always three of them - and he'd undone it without me knowing and taken it out. Of course that was why the man was standing in the way, so that the other passengers couldn't see what was going on, though this woman obviously did, she must have seen him undoing the straps at the back. It was real Dickens stuff, real pickpocket stuff. Of course when I'd got out, then I felt in my pocket, and my purse was gone, my passport was gone, so we were stranded.

We went up to some official because I had a bit of Spanish, and my wife could speak it quite well because she'd done A-level Spanish, so we went up to a railway employee and said, 'this has happened, what can we do?' Then a man in plain clothes came up and said 'I'll take you to the police station'. The police station was actually in the underground station and he waited there with us. We were sat down and a young woman took our names and addresses and wrote it all down. She spoke really good English and she said 'what do you call a person in England who doesn't get paid but helps people out, helps the police and the public but doesn't get paid' and she kept going on and on 'what's the name?' and we kept looking at each other and thinking 'what's she talking about?' Of course, this man who'd taken us to her was a vigilante, but he wanted to be paid. Of course, we didn't have any money because I'd lost it all, but he was waiting to be paid. It was a ridiculous situation, and they were all part of it, it's an incredible system out there.

We came out of the police station and walked back to the hotel. We told the hotel people what had happened and they were very nice about it. They'd obviously seen it time and time again, the metro station was right outside the hotel. So we didn't get to the museum.

They told us where the American and the British embassies were because although I'd finished academically at the college I wasn't leaving the house until the September when Mary arrived back from England, so all our stuff was in America, we'd left everything there, so we had to get back into America and of course the visa was in the passport.

We went to the British Embassy, now if you can imagine this British Embassy it was like a really big old Victorian house, very nice. The policeman-cum-soldier on the gate was very polite, there were big gates, no dogs, nothing like that, we just explained what had happened and they let us in. We went in and the people in the British embassy were very nice to us, they said 'don't worry, we'll get you a passport within about two or three days'. They gave us some money, set us up with a bank so we could draw money out, they were really really good to us. Then they said: 'you'll have to go and get a visa from the American embassy' and that's when our troubles started.

The American embassy was only just down the road from the British embassy. It was like Fort Knox, with a concrete wall around it about 10 foot high with barbed wire on the top and closed iron gates with nobody there. There were soldiers who didn't talk to you behind the gates in the compound, you had to ring a red telephone situated on the outside of the wall. So we phoned them up and they said 'well, you've got to start queuing for your visa at five o'clock in the morning because we're only open for an hour in the morning between nine and ten but people start queuing at five, so if you actually want to get your visa, you've got to start queuing at five o'clock'.

The first morning we went there, we got there about half past five in the morning and there was a queue about a mile long coming from the American Embassy. There was one window that was open for one hour a day; this is how they stop the Mexicans getting into America. Anyway, we queued up for a bit, for about three or four hours, and then everyone started dispersing, and that was it. Jo said 'tomorrow we'll have to get here earlier'. So we got there earlier the next day, it was just the same thing, we were still miles away from the American Embassy, so we stood in the queue just hoping. We did it for three days, and Jo said, 'I'm not doing this any more, this is bloody stupid'. She'd already gone to the telephone and said 'look, we're English, we're not Mexican'. Of course, the people on the other side, on the telephone, were Mexicans, so they couldn't care less who we were. It was just a nightmare.

When we were getting up at five o'clock in the morning, the people in the hotel wanted to know why we were getting up so early and going out, so we told them, and they said 'don't worry, we'll get you over the border, there's ways of getting you over the border back into America'.

I had to pick up my passport when it was ready so I went back into the British Embassy and I saw the attaché again and told him what had happened. And he said: 'oh no, this is ridiculous, I'll get you a visa' so he got onto the phone to them straight away and they said a visa will be there in about a week, and it did come. They didn't like it very much because I had a beard when I was in America, so I looked a bit like an older version of Che Geuvara or somebody! I've still got that passport and it's stamped with a Mexican stamp from Mexcio City.

So there was no visit to Oaxaca because we hadn't got the money, we'd lost all that, so we decided to stay in Mexico City, and that was really good, because there is such a lot to see in Mexico City. We went to the anthropology museum which is most probably the best in the world. Before the Spanish arrived, the Conquistadores, there were about twelve different cultures, but they weren't within the modern borders of Mexico, or Peru, or wherever, they just were the whole length of South America, there weren't these artificial boundaries there are now. You get Mayan culture going out of different countries into other countries, the Mayans, the Olmecs, the Incas, the Aztecs, it's incredible to see all these different cultures, some like the Olmec who I hadn't heard of before, who did these huge stone heads. The anthropology museum was fantastic, I think we spent a couple of days in there.

We went to see the Diego Rivera murals, there's a lot of murals in Mexico City, not just by him but others too, such as Siqueiros and Orozco. We went to visit the Frida Kahlo and Diego Rivera house, which is sort of an ultramarine colour, in the suburbs and you could tell they were very well looked after. Because one of the things we did notice was like I said the differences in lifestyle. Whenever we came out of the hotel there used to be a woman selling bits of cactus for one peso, I can't tell you what one peso is but it's absolutely nothing.

In the very poor area there was one street that I'll never forget because there was a whole street with Adana printing presses. Over here they used to have these little Adana printing presses which is like a circular plate, you have a handle and it comes down, you put the metal typeface in it and it comes down, well, they had enormous ones out there and they had them in the street and at night they would box them up. They stayed in the street, and they would do whatever printing you wanted, flysheets, marriages, births, change of address, little cards, they'd do whatever you wanted, and there were about twenty or thirty of these Adana printing presses down this street where you could get this done. They were enormous machines, and then at night they would box them up and go away and leave them there.

But of course in the expensive area, there were computers and everything, so you'd got two different communities almost, within the same city, and one thing we noticed, because some of the museums didn't have air conditioning, so they got really hot, you went through those quite quickly I'm afraid, but it was quite interesting seeing that too, because there was one museum we went to where there was a woman behind us sweeping up, with a little hand brush. Of course what they do is they try and employ all their relatives, and it is corrupt but in a funny sort of way it's not that bad, I mean, they're just trying to help each other. But it was quite an eye opener to how the Mexican system works.

But it was really good to walk around Mexico City and see it. We went to the zoo, which I thought was one of the best zoos I've ever been to, I've been to German zoos, Spanish zoos, English zoos, and it was a beautiful zoo, it's free, you don't have to pay, the animals have got all the space and you have got just tiny walkways. So it's not like London zoo where you've got massive walkways and tiny little cages. We noticed that the people we saw in the zoo were so respectful to the animals, there's no throwing peanuts at the animals like I witnessed in the zoo at Barcelona, or chewing gum, like I witnessed once at London zoo, they've got incredible respect and I was really impressed by that, the respect they had for the animals.

We went out to the Temple of the Sun and the Moon. My friend Nigel, who used to work in the department of archaeology at Lincoln in England, who used to work on archaeological sites, once told me just something of interest, that people historically have always just discarded their rubbish and every village would have a place where they would just throw the rubbish, they wouldn't even dig it into a hole. He said 'if you want to get pieces of pottery and stuff just have a look round and you'll find somewhere'. So Angie and I started scurrying around and trying to identify somewhere where, when they were building the pyramids, they might have discarded some of the stuff. Lo and behold we found a little mound, just a mound, and started kicking, because we couldn't be too obvious, we just started kicking some of the earth away. We found a tiny little flint which I've still got, a little tiny flint knife, about half an inch long and about a quarter of an inch wide, and it's been knapped, it's just the blade of the knife. We found a piece of ceramic too, and we went up the Temple of the Sun, which was incredible, because the steps are very high and they're very narrow, you have to go up sideways and my wife wouldn't do it, just me and my daughter. We went up to the top and it was fantastic, you got a real sense of what they achieved.

So we had a really good time in Mexico City, it wasn't wasted at all, and in fact it was better because we saw a lot of stuff that we wouldn't have had time for if we'd gone to Oaxaca. We went to the Museum of Modern Art which was another interesting place politically because obviously even in the 1960s/70s it was the thing for Mexico to be influenced by America, so there were all these big welded sculptures, very very similar to what David Smith was doing in the fifties and sixties, and of course it had all gone out of fashion because the political times had changed and they wanted to have their own identity. So all this stuff was left in the gardens where it used to be when it was brand new, but it had been left to literally rot, so because it wasn't made out of stainless steel it decayed, it rusted away, so you had to be a bit careful walking around the gardens, otherwise you might get a bit of sculpture on top of you. They were like skeletons of the 1960s, so it didn't please me too much seeing all this stuff but at the same time I understood there is always this tension, the European and Spanish and the Mexican. Of course that's what Diego Rivera was trying to do, because after all when Diego was in Paris he was doing cubist paintings, but when he went home he realised that he had to encompass the indigenous background, and that's what his mural's about, it's about modernising Mexico but also including the Indians and history in that.

Getting to realise all that was quite important to me, I think, and like I said we were very aware that we were tourists in a third world country. One of the things that brought it home to us, they had some really good cake shops in Mexico City, and every day Angie and I used to go together to this cake shop and I used to buy Angie a cake. Every time we got there, there was the same little boy sitting outside the cake shop, and I used to throw him some coins and we used to go in and buy a cake and come out again. He never smiled, he never did anything, nothing. About the third or fourth day we went in to buy a cake, it wasn't far from the hotel, it was just something, you know, she liked the cakes, about the third or the fourth day we were in the cake shop, and I'd already thrown him some coins and he'd never moved. Angie said, 'I wonder if the boy outside would like a cake Dad' so I said 'yeah, let's buy him a cake' so we bought him a cake and she gave him this cake. I've never seen anything like it, and she remembers it too, his face just lit up with this smile, and of course it suddenly dawned on me, he wasn't getting the money, it wasn't for him, it was a racket, like everything else in Mexico, but he got the cake and ate it!

We had a really good time in Mexico City, and I was impressed with Mexico. California was good too, but not as much as Mexico. As I said before, there were whole sides of America that I didn't like, and the culmination was the bit about me staying out there for 366 days. I'd seen Angie and Jo off on the plane on the 365th day and I went down to the airport on the 366th and they looked at my passport and they said: 'Your visa ran out yesterday' so I made up some excuse and they weren't too bad about it.

The plane took off and I suppose we'd got about half way to cloud level, when there was this almighty bang right near the seat. I was sitting right next to the window and the wing was in front of me, there was this mighty bang, and then there was about 15 feet of flames coming out of one of the engines. The woman next to me starts screaming, literally screaming her head off and I'm watching all this and thinking 'oh shit, what's going to happen now?' My hands started sweating, I'll never forget that, my hands started really sweating, they were almost completely covered in water, because I really did think this was it. I've never really had a problem with planes before, I didn't like flying at that time but I'd never really thought it was going to be my end.

The captain came on and he said 'we've got a slight problem'. I'll never forget that, 'we've got a slight problem'. It appears they had an automatic system in the engine that shuts the engine down, when they catch light, and just as he said that, lo and behold the flames stopped, but then we were only on three engines. He said: 'we can't fly to England on three engines so we are going to have to go back to San Francisco airport'. He'd left his intercom on, so you could hear him talking to San Francisco airport, and they were saying 'you can come back but the passengers can't get off the plane because they've gone through customs'.

We flew around and everybody was wondering when we were going to land. He came back on and said: 'we'll be about an hour circling around San Francisco airport'. I found out later that they'd had to jettison all the fuel because you can't land on full tanks, planes are too heavy to land on full tanks. So all that time there was this stuff like steam coming out of the end of the wings, which was fuel, and that was all dropping down to the people in San Francisco. Presumably this happens quite a lot.

In the end we got back and they kept us waiting four hours on the tarmac. There were children on the plane, and they were all screaming, the toilets were overflowing, it was ridiculous, and this was solely because we'd gone through customs, our visas had run out and they didn't want us back on American soil. It took them four hours to talk to the people that were in charge of the customs and immigration and to tell them that there was no way that they could transfer us to another plane. In the end we were let off and we were all delegated different hotels. I'd already phoned home by that time and told them what had happened, and I thought 'well, don't worry Douglas, you survived that, go down and have a beer'.

I went down to the hotel bar, and there was this man in uniform who happened to be the flight engineer. I didn't know anything about planes, we got talking and he told me about how planes work and it was him who told me what had happened with the fuel. Once they go up they can't come down without jettisoning that fuel, so in an emergency they've got a real problem because they've got to take the risk of coming down with those fuel tanks which might blow up on impact. I think that's what happened to the Concorde, when people were watching the Concorde they couldn't understand why the pilot didn't come down, he tried to keep it going, hoping he could put the fire out because he couldn't have landed and that's what happened, as soon as he landed it all burst into flames. I didn't realise there are four people in the cockpit, there's the navigator, the flight engineer, the co-pilot and the pilot, so I learned a lot through this and he said 'don't worry, you've been through it now, nothing else can go wrong, don't worry about it'.

There was no Virgin plane, I learned a lot, these airlines get their people on, the plane flies off to its destination, whether it's England or Spain or wherever and there are people on the other end wanting to come back on that plane so if you knock a plane out of service, Virgin obviously didn't have a spare plane. So we - the 200 or however many people were on board - were all given different flights and I was given one to Washington, on a United Airways plane. I was on this old 707 which was like the old planes that I'd flown to America on in the 70s, and it was shaking, and it no sooner took off than we had to land again because the cargo door hadn't closed. But eventually I got to Washington, and then I can't remember what happened - I think they'd negotiated me a seat on British Airways to get me back to Heathrow. A couple of weeks after that Virgin Atlantic sent me a letter saying 'we're sorry about the inconvenience and you've got a ticket to America if you want it' but it was only one way! So I've still got it, I've never used it, what's the good of a ticket for Douglas Jeal for just one way? Because I'd have to fork out to come back, and generally single flights are just as expensive as return.

Chapter 14 - Barcelona 1998-99

When I came back from California I went back to work at Anglia Polytechnic University (APU) to a nice studio that the university had given to Mary while she was exchanging with me. The sculpture department was in a place called Paradise Street in Cambridge, and we had the whole bottom floor and the top of a terraced house. They gave it to us as a studio because the health and safety people had said 'no you can't have 12 or 14 students in there because the floor won't take the weight'. Underneath was being used as student accommodation, so they were very worried about what went on the floor. So they gave it to me as a studio, because I was working in acrylic and not stone, and it enabled me to make the big acrylic things.

Most of the material came either from skips or it was off-cuts that I managed to buy cheaply, because acrylic is and always has been incredibly expensive. I used to travel around to different places to get it cheaper, because Cambridge isn't a very cheap place for acrylic or anything else. So a lot of the pieces were not designed and made like the aluminium pieces I did in the 1960s, they were driven by the materials I could get, and I tried out different things. The early ones, which I'd made when I was at Farm Cottage, were the lattice ones, where I left the paper on but cut it up into a lattice pattern. I retained that but also I sometimes used to tear it and sometimes paint it over the top with acrylic paint. I made about five or six in the period between coming back from California in 1995 and going to Barcelona in 1998. I mainly concentrated on these quite objective pieces that were to do with dance, including a piece called *Tango* which I did later when I came back from Barcelona. They were about movement and colour, and I was experimenting with using paint. I used paint on the acrylic differently from the way I do now, I used it primarily to soften the transparency down so that it became translucent but had a sort of pastel shade. I was quite interested in getting a pastel feel to it. And out of that came a different sort of approach - by the time we got to Barcelona I was thinking about using the acrylic sheets in another way.

The Barcelona trip came about because my wife had done her first year in print-making at Sonoma University where I was a Fulbright Scholar in sculpture, and when she came back she then did a year of Spanish and French at APU but she didn't want to be in the Fine Art department because that was where I was teaching. She got a place at Winchester, and she and Angie went to live in Winchester in student accommodation. We had a flat in Cambridge and I had the church and I had mortgages on both. I decided to try and buy something in Winchester and the only way I could do it was by selling the church, and putting a deposit on a house in Winchester and paying the mortgage down there. I didn't get very much for the church, I'd had the church quite a long time, I had it valued and it was worth another £20,000 to what I got for it because we had an economic downturn and I ended up getting only about £32,000 for it for all the time and effort. But that enabled me to buy a very nice 1930s house in Highcliffe in Winchester where Jo and Angie lived and I used to go down there every weekend.

Then Jo wanted to do an MA and we saw they were offering one in European Fine Art. I wrote off to Barcelona University because I knew them, and asked them if they had any Artist in Residence or anything like that I could do. They didn't, so I thought, well, I don't really want to be separated from my wife and daughter for a whole year, and I quite looked forward to living in Barcelona but I had to find the money. I wasn't earning a great deal at the college, and because I was part-time, they said they couldn't give me a sabbatical or anything like that, but they'd let me take it off without pay. I'd managed to save up about £10,000, plus we had rent income from the house in Winchester because we rented it out through an agency, which handled it really well, they were very good to us.

I decided to do the MA as well as Jo, and Anglia paid for half my fees for the MA. It seemed to be really a good idea for us to both be out there and for our daughter to go to a Catalan school. Although Angie was quite aggrieved about going to Catalan school, I think generally she liked it better than she'd liked the American school. She made friends quite easily I think considering the first day at school she didn't know any Catalan at all and virtually none of them spoke English at that age.

So we had money to live off for the year, but I needed to find a way of getting materials for my sculpture. I wrote off about fifty letters to acrylic suppliers, ICI, all sorts of people, to try and get support to get my material. At first I only got one letter back, from someone in Southampton saying ' I've got a few bits of scrap about 5 or 6 inches long, if you want to come down and take them out of the skip you're quite welcome' and I thought, is it worth me going down there, because I had to pack the van with all our stuff for a whole year, all our clothes and everything, I made a box to go into the roof rack, to take tools and materials.

Then the day before we were supposed to leave I got a letter from an international acrylic firm, Barlo International Plastics, saying they would agree to give me as much acrylic as I wanted, they weren't going to deliver it but I could collect it in Montaro, which is an industrial town outside Barcelona. I called the company, I could speak very little Spanish but I managed to negotiate and get what I wanted. And like an idiot I didn't think about it, I'd just asked for all this stuff, and if I'd thought about it I'd have asked for the coloured translucent, instead of that I'd just asked for the clear. They did give me some of the translucent, some coffee coloured sheets and some blue sheets which I asked for but most of it was clear because I thought I was going to paint on it.

I went to pick it up and there were about 50 huge sheets of plastic. I calculated that they probably gave me about £5,000 worth of stuff. They were in enormous sheets though, something like 12ft by 8ft, so when I got there I couldn't do anything with them because I'd got the van but I couldn't carry that sort of size on the roof rack. They grumbled a bit because I asked them to cut it all up for me, but they cut it up into reasonable sizes that I could get into the van, about 6ft to 8ft in length, and then it took me a couple of journeys to get it all back to the studio.

We had a really nice three bedroom flat which was actually cheaper to rent than the rent we got for the house in Winchester so we were gaining on that front, about a couple of hundred pounds a month. It was near the Arc de Triomf, very central and it wasn't far from Pep's place. I'd been to Barcelona so many times since 1988 that I knew where everything was so I knew where the cheap old-type supermarkets were. The indoor markets were fantastic, ours was Santa Caterina Market, the other time when I stayed in Florida Blanca the nearest indoor market was Sant Antoni Market.

The main art school was down by the Picasso museum where the print-making was, but I had a studio, not huge but it was a nice studio, in a big complex down by the Besos river. It was in an area where the nineteenth century artisan quarters were, very run down, all the leather works, carpenters, farriers, blacksmiths and all those people, and it had a lot of really good shops. Mariscal, the commercial artist and animator and cartoonist, who did the mascot for the 1992 Olympics, he had a big centre there with loads of people working for him.

I did a lot of work there and I think the amount of work that I did there I really enjoyed. I liked being with the other students but I was a lot older. There were a couple of other older students but I think I was the oldest, most of them were in their early twenties. But there were people like my wife and Rick, there were quite a few, four or five older students I suppose and it was good and there were the people who ran it themselves, Claudia Terstappen who was German, she was a photographer and Joe Milne who was a painter, good artists and there was a nice feel about it, it had a nice atmosphere, it was a really nice place. I didn't mind being a student again.

There were photographic facilities at the studio, so for the first time since the 1960s in the kitchen at Grange Road I was able to do photography again, but when I say photography I am not a photographer as such, it was very abstract photography for my work, taking shots of the sculpture I was making and then playing with that, superimposing them, getting different negatives off, sometimes putting three or four negatives in the enlarger, sort of a layering technique which I got into which has been quite useful to me right up to the present time. That was most probably one of the biggest things that came out my stay in Barcelona, as well as the influence from being in a very lively Mediterranean port.

I knew that I was going to work in acrylic before I went, and that I'd got this big sponsorship from Barlo International Plastics, so I'd been clever enough to take my tiny little band saw which was great because it enabled me to cut things up and all I had to do was get an adaptor for the plug to go into the Spanish system. I took quite a few tools because I knew the college wouldn't have tools because it wasn't a sculpture place, it was more of a print making and painting MA, so I took my tools with me, but I didn't have anything to bend the acrylic with. I asked Pep if he knew of any mechanical or electrical shop that would sell an acrylic bender and he didn't know where I could get one. I started looking and I realised I was spending a lot of time on it. If you're going to a new city you've got to find things, and although I knew Barcelona culturally and knew about food and stuff I didn't know where to get those sort of material things, in fact just the trip to get the material turned into a whole day because I had to go to a completely new town that I'd never been to on this industrial estate and find it. So everything took much longer than I'd expected and I was very aware that I'd only got a year out there, so in the end I thought I'd just go and buy an electric fire. I knew the name for an electric fire, *estufa*, so I went into a shop and asked for one, but he didn't quite understand me, and I hate pointing, because you see English abroad pointing, so I drew little drawings of what I wanted and this man came out with an electric fire which I've still got and I'm still using in my workshop. I took the grate off this Spanish electric fire and adapted it, and it wasn't great but it worked perfectly all right for what I wanted to do. When I think of the amount of work that I did, it was incredible that I did it with this tiny little one-bar electric fire.

I started making sculpture, I made a mobile which I didn't really like very much, and it's been packed up for the last 11-12 years, although if I unpacked it I'd probably find it's quite interesting. I've got one black and white photograph of it, and when I was looking at it the other day I thought, hmm, it looks a bit like a lot of the work I'm doing at the moment, so it'll be quite interesting one day when I unpack it, but I don't really like the idea of mobiles. It was more of a hanging piece, about 6ft tall and it just hung and just skipped off the ground.

Then I did a thing which was later to become the piece which was at the Institute of Astronomy called *Inside Out*. It was very strange being out there because I had the use of photography when I was a post-graduate student at St Martin's and a lot of the way I started thinking again was like what I'd done at St Martin's when I was 19-20. One of the projects that Anthony Caro had given us when I was a student was *Inside Out* and I started thinking about it again, and I also started thinking about Fellini's *Eight and a Half*. I must have seen the film in London in the late 1960s early 1970s, and it suddenly came back to mind that here was a guy who was very successful at making films and they kept showering him with money to make films and then he ran out of ideas and so he made a film about making a film. And suddenly I got this idea about using photography, I'm taking pictures of making a sculpture, not me making it but actually every bit that's done and then I've superimposed it, layering it on itself so why don't I make the sculpture like that and make it all part of the process? So then I started to think of ways in which I could put the negatives onto the sculpture itself.

I had to go every day from the flat by the Arc de Triomf to drop Angie off at the Catalan school, and then along the coast for a couple of miles to the Besos River, so it was quite a journey. In the beginning I used to drop Angie off at the school and catch the bus, I liked the bus and I've it a lot in Barcelona because you see so much, but I got a bit tired of the bus and there was quite a walk from the studio to the bus stop so I thought, well, I'll get a bike. I could cycle along the promenade to the studio which was 15-20 minutes away. So I invested in a second hand racing bike, it was a lovely bike and I've still got it, but it was a bit of a disaster in one respect because of the toe clips.

We got there in the early summer and started work and by about September I invested in this cycle and forgot that because it was still hot I'd got sandals on. I pulled up at the traffic lights and I couldn't get my feet out because the sandal straps got caught in the toe clips. I just fell over sideways, because I couldn't get either foot off the bike. There wasn't a car or anything there that I could fall against so I actually fell all the way down, I put my arm out to stop myself hitting the ground, and I broke my wrist.

I had to go to hospital and have them sort my wrist out which they did do, it was fantastic actually, there was no hanging around for hours, in and sorted and very friendly and lovely about it. Angie had seen inside of a couple of hospitals over the time we'd been going to Barcelona, and every time they were always incredible, always really good service and lovely people. The Spanish are really nice people, I found everywhere.

There's not much they can do when you break your wrist because there are so many little bones. They put it in, not plaster but they put it in something to keep it straight. That was all right, it wasn't a big problem and it wasn't painful at all compared to later when I fractured my femur. I'd got a wrist problem but I still went to work

When they did it all they gave me the x-rays, they said 'here you are, we don't want them, they're no good to us' so I then thought, I had all these photocopies and transparencies and my x-rays so I started to think about how I could use the x-rays in my work. They were only of my wrist but it was quite interesting, because of all the little bones. I don't think I put an x-ray on *Inside Out* in the end because they were too thick, what I should have done was photocopy them off onto transparencies, but it gave me the idea. But it was quite exciting for me making *Inside Out,* and I don't think I would have done it unless I'd gone to Barcelona and had the photography facilities, so it sort of changed my ideas.

The other thing that changed my ideas, although I didn't realise at the time, was that subconsciously the Mediterranean was filtering through to me, because it's very beautiful there and even in the winter Barcelona's very beautiful. And people use the beach, it's got a beach which has always been used. I've got photographs of Barcelona in the 1930s and you see all the people on the beach. There's not many places where there's a big city that's got a beach- it's a bit like Brighton in that respect I suppose. Admittedly since the 1990s they ship the sand in, they actually bring clean sand in but they've cleaned up that part of the Med, the sewage and everything, so it's quite nice there.

I'd ordered some transparent blue acrylic sheet, a lovely blue, a really really nice blue, I find it sort of succulent, and I used it to make this piece to go on the floor called *Water,* it's not very big, only about 4-5ft in diameter, but I was really pleased with it.

I'd also got some coffee coloured transparent acrylic, and I made quite a big installation piece out of that. I showed all this work at a place called Can Felipa, we had an exhibition there, and some of it I showed when I came back home. But it started me thinking in different sorts of ways about my work. I suppose altogether I got about four or five sculptures done in the year I was out there. I also did a bit of etching and so it was quite interesting for me to try out different things, which later led on to *Escrito de Campo* and *Callitactil*.

While I was in Barcelona in 1999 I met Gustav Metzger again, the auto-destructive artist whom I'd known at St Martin's in 1965. We were at a private view of *Action*, an exhibition at the MACBA, the Museum of Modern Art in Barcelona, an American exhibition on action painting, basically centred on Jackson Pollock's work. Gustav had got some pieces in there, although his action painting was to destroy the paintings he made with acid, autodestructive art. But the incredible thing is he looked the same in 1999 as he did in 1965.

He bounded over to me at the private view and said 'hallo Douglas', now we're talking about a man who must have been seventy something, but he remembered me from when he came in to St Martin's, which must have been when I was there, between 1962 and 1965 so we're talking about over 30 years earlier, almost 40, and he remembered me. Now that's incredible because I find it really really difficult to remember my students, it's always the good students and the bad students who stick out, the mediocre ones, you don't remember. I have got some students that go back nearly as far as that who I remember, but it is unusual. He was dressed in the same clothes, when he was at St Martin's I remember this light coloured suede jacket, a kind of orangey brown, and he still had that on when I met him, well it may not have been the same jacket, obviously, but it was the same style.

So I recognised him and he recognised me straight away and he gave me a name to check down at the Tate because he wasn't sure when we did this auto-destructive art at the Hayward Gallery, where he threw acid at one of his canvases, and he wanted me to go and talk to a woman there. Actually I never did, I should have done really because it was part of an archive she was trying to put together either about St Martin's or him, I don't know which.

I was eager to get back to Cambridge but then unfortunately my marriage started falling apart and I realised that my wife had got another apartment which I was paying for in Barcelona where she was entertaining a member of staff from Winchester School of Art. She was acting very strange, staying out late at night and sort of reverting back to being a teenager, wearing clothes that teenagers wear. There was something going on which I didn't understand and then at Christmas she became very ill. She had an awful temperature, I've never seen anything like it and I was very worried and really quite annoyed with her because she wouldn't go to the doctor's. I realised I was going to have to deal with this woman because she wouldn't let me anywhere near her but she was really ill and the temperature was so high she was having fits, her whole body would go into spasms. For two days I nursed her and put ice packs on her and got her temperature down and she was screaming at me 'leave me alone', it was horrible. I didn't really understand so when she got better there was a distance between us because of this but I didn't know anything about the flat at that time.

We were still living together and I came home one day, I can't remember how it happened but I saw some letters this chap had written. Then in May I found this envelope addressed to her from him and I confronted her with it. Of course she denied it at first and then she said it was a student and then this person and that person. It was all rather silly really, she wasn't upset, she got very adamant that I shouldn't know, she didn't want to talk about it in any way which made it very difficult for me because it meant that there was no way we could be reconciled.

It ended up one night with her saying to Angie 'come on, you're coming with me, we're leaving Dad' and that's when I found out she really had got her own place and Angie said 'no, I'm not going, I'm really not going'. She'd put Angie in a bit of a predicament because she was 11, and talking to her now she's grown up now, she's told me that her mum actually took her to the other place, so she knew about it, but she was sworn to secrecy not to tell me. And she said: 'I didn't want to live there anyway, I didn't want to leave you, I didn't want to live there with Mum'. So that was a bit of a shock, from May until we left Barcelona, Angie was living with me and that was that. In a way, it set the pattern.

I just got on with my work, I was very emotionally upset, and the people in Barcelona were all very nice to me, Joe Milne was and Claudia Terstappen, the Head of Fine Art at the place where I was studying. They were all very nice and helpful to me, but I was quite shocked at how emotionally upset I was. I carried on working and got things done, cooked for Angie, and generally it was okay. It was a difficult time, but it didn't spoil Barcelona for me, though it was traumatic and of course when you're in that situation it's dire but now looking back you realise how silly it all was, the mistakes she made. I suppose I really wanted her to talk to me about it like I'd done to her earlier, when I'd had been attracted to the Chinese girl before we went to Sonoma. I'd actually come out with it and we'd talked about it and I suppose I expected that from her, but she wasn't in that frame of mind. To be honest with you I think the marriage was just in the way of something that was happening with her, I don't think she dealt with Barcelona in a particularly good way, she'd sort of reverted back to being a teenager, she wanted to go out and stay up late, I don't know if she was on drugs or anything or what, I had no way of knowing.

Chapter 15 - Divorce and After 1999-2005

When we got back Angie was living with her mum in Winchester at first, because I had nowhere to live, so when I started back teaching at APU, I had to be very quick in finding us a place. I found a little terraced house in Castle Hill in Cambridge and got Angie into secondary school and of course I inherited the studio back at college. Then I just got on with trying to work out what had happened between my wife and me.

At first I tried for us to go to Relate but that didn't work, it was impossible to communicate with her because if she did communicate she lied which is often the case, it's done out of defence, I'm not trying to be nasty to her. It was absolutely impossible and I just sat there and thought, well, just hold on Douglas just stay here for a bit. I think Angie and I were in the place in Castle Hill for about two years altogether. I started to instigate divorce proceedings and it took two years. My wife was quite nasty in the beginning, she tried to say things about me which just weren't true, but in the end that was dropped, partly because Angie was spending most of her time with me, so as my solicitor rightly said if she's trying to make you out so horrible why isn't she trying to reclaim her daughter?

The solicitor at first said that I ought to do something about legally adopting Angie to safeguard myself, but there were two things on my mind about that. Firstly, mothers and children can't really be separated, Angie loves her mother no matter what, and you do love your children no matter what, even if they're murderers, so I didn't really want to put a wedge between her and her mother, and also, I didn't want her mother to be even more awkward than she was being. I wasn't frightened of her because I felt that I was in the right, not because she'd committed adultery, I don't mean like that, if she'd been willing to talk about it I'd have been willing to forget. I don't think it was a problem, for me personally. I was well into my fifties, and although it hurt me that she'd gone off with another man, that wasn't the big deal, I could have forgiven that. It was just that, with all relationships there's that point where you either talk about it, and work it out, or you don't, and she wasn't in a position where she wanted to do that. I think that's quite crucial, because a friend of mine said, 'look Douglas, you can try Relate, you can try all these things, but I've talked to her, and I think she's made up her mind to go so she's going to go and there's nothing you can do'. There are times when couples can actually get over their differences and live together and carry on, but I think if one of the people has made up their mind to go there's nothing you can do really. And that's what I felt, that she'd made up her mind, she'd changed her lifestyle, she didn't want my lifestyle any more, or she didn't want the lifestyle we had together. She'd had Angie very young, so she hadn't had much of a life when she was younger so I could see that she was replaying that, if you like, that she wanted to be a twenty year old again. I suppose at that point in time I realised that the most important thing was not to antagonise the situation.

In a way too, like all people that go through these break ups, in some ways it was very secure for me because I'd got money, I'd got my income, I was renting a house, I was looking after my daughter. She saw her mum at weekends and it was okay, and then Jo managed to get a flat that was quite close to us so she could see more of Angie. Angie was at my house for about four or five days a week and she was seeing her mum about two or three days a week and that's the way it went on. I didn't mind that, I'd got my own place and Angie was there most of the time. When you've got a child with you most of the time you're thinking about feeding them, getting them off to school, the different things going on with her. We went off on holiday a lot together, Christmas, Easters and summers, we went off with friends. I was just trying to deal with the divorce, but otherwise I felt, and I think looking back it's true, I was functioning perfectly normally. I have this funny thing, I always make art no matter what, it's a bit like that stage thing, the actor goes on stage even though he's just lost his wife or something, you just get on with it. It's not heroic, it's just it keeps you sane, and it keeps you concentrating on something, you don't get in a silly situation where you're just thinking about it all the time and going round in circles. There were times when I was on my own, like when Angie went to see her mum at weekends, but I'd got friends that I went to see, and as often happens I had a male friend who was in a very similar situation so we used to go to the pub and have a drink. But most of the time I was getting on with teaching, that preoccupied me four days a week, I was doing my own work, so I didn't have much time to spare. And we had some really good holidays together, me and Angie. We used to be invited by people, because I suppose they felt sorry for us.

I got back and started working in the studio. A gallery director from Brick Lane in London got in touch with me and said would I like to meet, because he had seen my work, I don't know quite how, but he was very interested in my work and what I was doing. He'd seen pictures of *Water, Inside Out* and some other pieces. The Institute of Astronomy had taken *Inside Out* for inside their building, so a lot was beginning to happen for me.

I went up to see the gallery in London - Gallery 99 I think it was called, it was an incredible building, and they showed me what they were offering me which was enormous gallery space, a beautiful wide gallery, just off Brick Lane. At that time - 2000 - Brick Lane wasn't as well known as it is now but it was just starting to take off and it was lovely for me and Angie, because she went up there with me. From living in America we both love bagels and salt beef and of course at that time there were loads of bagel and salt beef places down Brick Lane because it was still a very working-class area. It's not now, it's turned into something completely different.

He offered me an exhibition there, and again lots of subconscious stuff had begun. Things take time to come out and you don't realise what's going on at the time. Obviously now looking back at the divorce I feel it was influencing me in some ways, and looking after my daughter and that strong relationship that we had, because we always had had a very close relationship, me and Angie, which is strange when you think biologically she's not mine, but I am her father because she's never known anybody else.

I'd done the photographs when I was in Barcelona and I got very interested in thinking about how I could get images on to clear or translucent acrylic. The piece at the Institute of Astronomy had transparent photocopies taped on with double sided sticky tape, but I knew that wasn't a good way of doing it, because sooner or later the double sided tape would dry up and become brittle and then the images would come off. That was what happened and I had to take it away from the Institute a couple of years ago. I knew that I had to solve that problem if I wanted to put images on the acrylic. One way would have been to silk screen them on, but I don't like silk screen at all, I didn't want to do it with silk screen, so I started experimenting with other ways of doing it.

Towards the end of Barcelona I remembered back to when Wa was teaching me Chinese calligraphy in the middle of the 1990s, and I thought that I could cut out the calligraphic Chinese shapes and bend them and then hang them. I'd got an acrylic that was a charcoal colour, like ink, so I wanted to use it for calligraphic shapes. Even before I knew Wa, dating back to the 1960s, I was always a reader of poetry. Even when I was first at college, I started reading TS Eliot, Dylan Thomas, James Joyce, Ted Hughes, Douglas Dunn and people like that. Also Sylvia Plath was a great interest of mine when I was in my twenties. So I'd always had this relationship with the written and poetical word, and when I got into reading about Zen in the late 1960s there were things that I took on board that with Zen poetry there are not only puns on the sounds, but there are puns on the visual imagery that the characters are made up of. We don't understand that in the West so much but there are these linking elements so I thought, well, these pieces don't have to read as a piece of poetry, I can make them a visual poem about shapes.

So I started cutting out calligraphic shapes and bending them, but I didn't like them. The trouble is that the characters are too much of an art product in themselves. These are characters that over millennia have been changed slightly to arrive at the Chinese characters used today, and the poets didn't stick completely to the characters anyway, they did the brush strokes, and it was more like a kind of abstract expressionism. It's funny that the abstract expressionists were influenced by things like Zen and calligraphic shapes because they do get quite refined aesthetically, it's not just like doing the letter A or letter B or so on.

When this wouldn't work out, what I decided to do next was take an A4 sized sheet, draw some shapes on it and then bend them and see. The shapes weren't exactly organic, they were quite rounded cut-out shapes but then I bent them with the one bar electric fire which meant they were bent on themselves like an envelope. I made all these shapes and then hung them like a poem, I called it *Callitactil* and I'd shown that in Barcelona before I had the exhibition in London.

So when I got to London, I'd already hung them like an oriental poem, and I thought, no, I don't want to do that again, what shall I do? I'd only got about 36 or something of these shapes to hang like a poem. I'd got about nine months before the exhibition so I thought, I'll make some more of these shapes and then cover the wall with them, two walls, like a right angle, and don't keep to the strict poetry thing, just put these shapes in relationship to each other as an installation on the two walls of the gallery. And that's what I did. It was a successful show, but unfortunately no other show came out of it. I thought he liked the show, but the gallery closed down a year or so later. But anyway it was interesting, we had a good time up there, Angie and I. But then when I got the photos back - some professional photographer had done them, I can't remember who - looking at them I felt that the close-ups were ok but when the two walls were photographed it looked like a load of squashed flies all over the walls and I thought 'well I won't do that arrangement again'.

I got them back into my studio and decided then 'I've had enough of these, I'll pack them away' and so I started putting bubble wrap around them and packing them in cardboard boxes like I do when I'm really fed up with something. I thought 'well it's time to clear up the studio and get on with something else' and when I was tidying up the studio I found all these paper templates which I had drawn round and when I'd used them I just used to screw them up and throw them on the floor. There was a big grey piece of paper on the floor, and I suddenly saw these screwed up bits of paper on top of the grey background, and it came to me that these were like letters, screwed up letters or words on a flat surface. I'm a great believer in metaphor, Shakespeare was a fantastic person for metaphor, he gets two ideas, puts them together and you get something really original out of them. So here were some screwed up bits of paper on a grey floor and I just thought, a field of writing. Now I think I got it wrong, I called it *Escrito de Campo*, which I took to be Spanish for *Field of Writing*, but I'm not so sure now that it's right, I think it doesn't work like that, but that's what I called it.

What I did is take the same format, make some new proformas, and drew those onto the acrylic. And then I thought, 'no, I'm not going to bend these like I bent the other ones, I want to make them much more organic' because the paper shapes were screwed up like a ball, and of course they wouldn't have been a ball if I'd used this envelope method of just bending them straight. I invested in a pair of asbestos gloves and then heated the whole under a heater like a grill, I managed to heat the whole shape up, flat, and when it had gone floppy, picked it up with the asbestos gloves and made a ball shape. That's what I did with the fifty-odd or whatever is in *Escrito de Campo*, so there are fifty organic shapes squashed in on themselves like little balls. Then the idea was to have slate to put them on, a big slate rectangle as big as a room, but of course I couldn't afford slate, slate is very expensive, not only that it would be incredibly heavy. So I got some mdf and painted it slate colour, really well, and then put these pieces on 'slate' and I thought that was successful too, that was *Escrito de Campo*.

All the time there's this subconscious that's regurgitating things, you don't really know consciously what you're doing, but I think you do know subconsciously. It's that way with artists, writers, everybody, it's intuitive, you just know when something is working, and this certainly worked, like *Water*. I think the piece called *Water* worked really well, when I was in Barcelona, and *Escrito de Campo* really does work, there's something about it, and when the light comes through on the clear acrylic you get these shadows on the base.

I started thinking about different ways in which I could do pieces which were different from the painted pieces that I'd done earlier, the big sculptures which I'd done between the time of coming back from America and going off to Barcelona. I had a different way of working now which was much more to do with very small pieces, although I did make a couple of bigger pieces, one called *Tango* which I quite liked, which was a big painted piece, about 4 foot 6, which I've still got. The movement of it reminded me of tango, just the way that it moves. All the time in sculpture there's the stance, the movement, it's not just a question of doing a figure with two arms, two legs, you've got to think how you can make this figure much more interesting, almost just communicate the same movement in itself.

Over the history of sculpture you can see this. A great eye-opener is the Egyptian sculpture, in early times the format was that one leg had to be in front of the other, the arms by the side, and the face looking straight ahead, but when a new regime came in with Tutankhamen and that period, suddenly you get much more realistic sculpture, like the bust of Queen Nefertiti. So they were capable of it, it's just that that much more liberal atmosphere was needed to bring it out. Then with the Greeks and Romans, they didn't have the technical expertise to treat the marble like it was treated in the Renaissance, they used to have a tree stump or something coming up to support the leg or an arm or whatever. But by the Renaissance, technology had moved on and they'd got much more skilful so they could make things that were much more exciting to look at, just putting the head to one side rather than straight on.

So always there's the stance, and you can see that reflected in Degas' *Arabesque* and his dancing sculptures and also in the lovely little horse sculptures that he did and the smaller Rodins, the modelling of Rodin is amazing, and his portraits. Always it's to do with using the material in a way that isn't just descriptive, it's giving you something else. So I tried to do this with things like *Tango,* to give it a certain sort of movement and then to combine a title with it so that you understand what it's about, because a title is there to point you in the direction, to tell you how to see it.

I'd had a good reaction to the exhibition in Brick Lane, the people who went to see it said it was good, I didn't have any press coverage apart from a little bit that the gallery themselves had arranged, and then I was hoping that something else would come out of that, and I suppose in a way some things did, but not as much as I would have liked. It was a very strange period because now looking back I can see that that time was to completely reshape my life. I was living in a house overlooking a graveyard in Bermuda Terrace in the north of Cambridge, with my daughter, she was with me most of the time. Most of my work was stored in the garage or in a big warehouse belonging to my ex in-laws, who had a furniture business and furniture shop in Peterborough at that time. I was quite happy with that because it was nice and dry, it was a good place for it to be, so things looked positive. My daughter was in a school which she didn't really like and I tried to get her into another school and was successful but then she didn't want to move because she'd already settled in.

We were seeing a friend of my ex-wife who we'd known since we were all living in Cherry Hinton and she was married to another sculptor who was called Tony Berlotti, but their marriage broke up some time earlier, when Jo and I got married. She became a good friend and Angie and I had some really good holidays with her and her children, we went to Collioure in the south of France, so at that time I was quite optimistic about things. The friendship broke down because I think she wanted more and like all those situations when you're raw from coming out of a relationship that you didn't actually want to finish I wasn't really ready for another relationship. I didn't know at the time what I know now, that I would spend so long on my own, whereas in the past, I'd had only small gaps of being single between relationships. So that was becoming a complete change to be on my own but I had my daughter and I had my studio at the university that I could work in so I had no problems other than that I couldn't really get my hands on the money until the divorce came through. I couldn't pay her off the money that she wanted from the house and I couldn't begin to buy another house and I was paying £700-800 a month just renting a very tiny house for me and my daughter. It was a little terraced house like the one that I lived in with my parents, a two-up-two-down, you walked straight into the living room, there was no hallway, and a tiny little yard as a garden and a garage which leaked, so it was good that I didn't have any really important work there.

After two or three years the divorce went through and I bought the house in Sawston, south of Cambridge, where I'm still living now. It coincided with Angie going to Sixth Form College on this side of Cambridge, so it was much easier for me to run her in and go to work and pick her up. I bought her a little scooter which was stolen which was a shame and then we had problems with the insurance, they didn't pay out so we lost the money. It was brand new and it was found completely mangled up. She lost it going to see her mum who was living in another part of Cambridge by then, and it was stolen from inside her mother's garden. It was quite a nasty experience, I think she really knew who did it, and I think she was a little terrified so I didn't really want to push her. I ended up trying to teach her to drive, which we never really got through because by that time she got into King's College, University of London to study geography.

About that time I started doing a series of paintings which were in a way autobiographical. They started off with a photograph I'd seen of a woman naked, a French photograph of a woman smoking in bed. And I liked the photograph, it's one of those photographs you see and I was thinking: 'why do I like this photograph so much, is it because it's a nude woman?' and that wasn't it at all, it wasn't erotic, and then I suddenly realised that she looked like my mother when I was young, she had long brown hair and I thought 'that could have been my mother when she'd conceived me'. I did a painting of it and that started me off. Eventually I had 24 paintings, which I called *Evocations*. They didn't correspond to years, they just corresponded to times in my life and they were a mixture of abstracts and figurative paintings. There was a really nice one I think on *Liberty, Fraternity and Equality* which a woman from Cambridge University Press bought for her office. I liked some of them more than others.

I had an exhibition of *Evocations* at Clare Hall, which is part of Cambridge University. It was the first time really that I'd shown any paintings. I'd shown some paintings in the first exhibition I'd had at Grabowski's in the 1960s because then I used to use the paintings as ideas for sculptures and then make the sculptures out of the paintings, three-dimensionally, but they were geometric and flat colour, whereas *Evocations* were much more painterly and like I said some were figurative. Clare Hall actually chose a piece called *The Dance* which I personally don't think was that good, it reminded me too much of Matisse's *Dance*, but it was their choice. But one of the things that I do enjoy is dance so it was talking about that.

So that was quite a nice little exhibition and as far as personal life, my daughter had left for university and that was quite strange because it was the first time I was really on my own and it took me some getting used to, not having somebody around the house. Sometimes she used to come home for weekends, and I used to go up and see her, and we had some really nice times because when I was at St Martin's I really did like Central London and there were lots of places that I knew that she didn't know. We walked all over the City and I showed her Pudding Lane and all the rest of it, it's still there, hidden away behind all the high-rises, like the Monument is dwarfed by all these huge blocks now, but it's still there. We had some really lovely times, they'd just opened up that walk, you can walk all the way down from Tate Modern all the way down to Docklands along that side and that was fantastic. Angie lived at Borough Green, near Borough Market.

So we had some good times but I did miss her. I found it was all right in the summer, and I still do now, because you can go out in the evenings, but what I find dreadful is the winter months because you're stuck in, because I'm not somebody who watches television, I've had no television now for a couple of years. It was the first time I'd really thought 'Oh God I don't like this, I'm really on my own' and I'd had one or two attempts at affairs which just didn't work out, and it was my fault they didn't work out. I suddenly realised that in a way looking back, because I was the only child until the age of nine or ten, I have been on my own a long time. I hadn't always been in relationships because there were often one or two years between those relationships when I was on my own. And suddenly I realised that I do like being on my own and the fact is that I've done more work in the last ten years, although I was working as a lecturer four days a week up until 2010, I've still done more work than I ever did before. It's only comparable with when I left St Martin's and I'd done enough sculpture not to work for a year or so. So in that way I like the solo bit, and often when I go to the pictures and exhibitions I like being on my own because I like writing down stuff, my observations of the exhibitions, in notebooks. I was very sad just recently when I came back from Barcelona that I'd lost my notebook because this book covered about a year and a half, it covered the period when I was ill and everything.

The *Evocations* exhibition was a nice little exhibition, and around that time I was also making a lot of the painted acrylic pieces, *Tango* etc. I was just beginning to work on the pieces that were to become the *Codex*. At that time I didn't even know it was going to be called *Codex*, I started like I did with *Callitactil* and *Field of Writing*, I had the same format, the same shape and size, just a bit smaller than A4 and I started cutting out shapes. After I'd cut out about 15 or something and polished them, I wasn't quite sure at that point how to bend them, but I thought: 'these remind me of something'. I've always started to just draw shapes in a sketch book, and see where that will take me, and I started to come up with these very unusual shapes. It suddenly dawned on me that the shapes I was drawing reminded me a bit of the shapes I'd seen in Central American architecture and art.

When I was in Mexico I was very impressed by the Museum of Anthropology in Mexico City. I'd seen some of the work from the Americas but I really didn't understand till then the way that the countries were broken up by Portugal and Spain and that these cultures didn't have the same boundaries as there are today. There were twelve huge cultures, the Olmec, the Maya, the Inca, the Aztec, there were twelve of them altogether I was very impressed by seeing this, it's a beautiful museum, probably the best in the world I think, and it displays all these different cultures. Not only did I see some links between them but I saw links between the surviving codices (there's not many of those because the Spanish destroyed a lot of them). And in their stone sculpture, the shapes were the same, and some of the architecture, the way the stones knitted together and the way that they'd been placed. I was really interested in that, but as happens I didn't know at the time that that had had such a subconscious influence on me.

I was fascinated by the relationship between the written codices and the sculpture, the way they put the sculptural forms together. They used the same pictorial language, the way the sculpture's made is very blocked and stony and the way the codices are drawn is very blocked and stony and somehow that started to manifest itself when I was making these pieces. They weren't exactly the same shapes but they were my subconscious interpretation of those shapes. I was also thinking about how I could slot these things together, I was interested in the way that the stone in Central American architecture is slotted together, I didn't actually want to do that but I wanted to slide it together somehow.

In the 1970s I'd made a piece of sculpture called *Envelope,* unfortunately it got destroyed, but it was the first time that instead of sticking a piece together I'd connected it by slotting it together like an envelope. I'd got these pieces, so I tried folding them and then slotted them together in pairs. Then

I thought well, it would be good if there was something on them, literature or something. That was when I got the idea of using them as a codex, to tell a pictorial story with a three-dimensional shape. And just as the paintings in the *Evocations* series had in a way told the story of my life so far, I decided to create a *Codex* which would tell the history of the twentieth century.

I started gathering together lots of photographs of things that meant a lot to me, and also experimenting with different ways of transferring images onto the acrylic sheets. I'd already done that with *Inside Out* and ended up sticking them on with double sided tape, which lasted for about ten years but then started peeling off. I experimented with different glues and things and in the end came up with using a kind of liquid acrylic. You mix two chemicals together and it makes a terrible stink. I'd used it before but the problem with it is if you stick two pieces of acrylic with it and then drop the combined piece, it's such a good bond, that it won't break where you've them stuck together, but it'll break somewhere else. So I don't use it much on the small constructions, the wall pieces and the three-dimensional pieces, because if you do drop them they actually break at the join and they can be stuck back together again, but if they're too well stuck the material will shatter instead because they're quite fragile, so I don't use this glue much.

I found out through experimentation that if I squeegee some of this glue on then stick the photocopy to it ink down, it sticks to the acrylic and then I caught the corner of one of the photocopies sticking out and was amazed that I could pull off the plastic from the photocopy leaving the ink embedded in the resin, the actual ink had been imprinted into the liquid acrylic and the ordinary transparency from the photocopy just fell off. It didn't do it perfectly because you have to get it very smooth, if you push the ink too much then the ink starts to smear so you've got to be very careful, sometimes it breaks the image up, but I quite liked the smearing effect. Rather than being a perfect reproduction all the time it gave me lots of accidental things, and I quite like that, so now I'm using that effect as a thing in itself.

So that's what I do now, I squeegee the glue on, press the image into the glue and when it's dry peel off the backing. Then I bent them like an envelope, instead of sticking I used two shapes bent back on themselves and slipped into each other, so that I had two images on each if you like 'word' of the codex.

Chapter 16 - Poland 2006-08

While I was in the process of working out how to transfer the images to the acrylic and create the pieces for the *Codex*, I received a letter from a woman called Pauline Kirk, the curator of the Łódź Museum of Modern Art in Poland, saying that they owned a piece of my sculpture and would I go and restore it, because it was in a bad way. They said 'you don't have to pay for anything, we'll pay for the flight and we'll put you up at the museum'.

I wasn't apprehensive, I was just amazed. For a start, I didn't know that they owned a piece of my sculpture, so I was a bit shocked about that, because the Łódź Museum was one of the first museums of modern art in the 1930s. Łódź was a very industrial place, especially in textiles, but also a lot of artists collected there, in particular the modernists, Wladyslaw Strzeminski and Katarzyna Kobro, people like that, although I didn't really know any of this when I first went there. I knew of Kobro because I'd come across her after St Martin's, and her metal pieces were sort of similar to the pieces that I did after I left St Martin's, one of which was the piece they owned. So when I got there it was quite a shock to know that this museum was in its heyday in the 1930s as being at the centre of Modernism outside of Russia along with the Bauhaus. Łódź is also famous for the film school, with people like Wajda and Kieślowski.

Łódź is a strange city because like I said it was obviously in its heyday before the Second World War, it's very much like our Manchester with red brick textile factories which are incredibly big, and huge working class estates which are nothing like what we put up. They're fantastic buildings, they're terraced houses but they're much better build, they're much better to look at, they're all built on a square so you get a square of terraced houses with one side that faces the road and then in the middle you have grass and trees and places for the children to play. There are row after row of these squares, and with each square there's an opening in the front which has wrought iron gates and an archway over the gate. It's all very well done, and then of course in this complex there are schools.

I think there were between eight or twelve giant textile manufacturers in Łódź, and they all put up their own premises for their workers, but all much the same. I wouldn't say it was anywhere near as hard as Manchester and our Midlands places, and certainly they seemed to have a better lifestyle. I don't know what it was like inside the factories, the factories were enormous and they were textile factories right up until the Second World War. Then the Germans took them over and used them to manufacture German uniforms, most of the factories were owned by the Poles, there were about three or four that were owned by Jews and of course that all went when the Nazis came. After the Germans left the Russians took them over exactly the same, but of course once the Russians went all these buildings became derelict because the Poles hadn't got enough money to run them themselves, there was no private enterprise at that time, or perhaps there was no incentive any more to do industrial textiles. There was no market for them because they were just making Soviet uniforms as far as I know. So you have all these huge buildings which were left to rot. Łódź had really declined, you have about eight to ten Art Nouveau houses in Łódź which are actually falling to pieces, really falling to pieces because there was no money or no will to restore them.

By the time I got to the Museum there were plans ahead and most probably the museum has moved into one of these factories by now. There was one that they were restoring when I was there the first time, a huge complex called Manufaktura.

I arrived at the airport, which is quite interesting because it's got such a short runway that as soon as you touch down, the pilot has to pull on his brakes otherwise you'd overshoot the runway. It's quite a frightening experience, but in fact the last time I went there they were actually lengthening the runway.

I got there at about ten o'clock in the evening, and it was the winter, it was about 15° to 20°C below zero and I hadn't really understood that it was going to be so cold. I didn't know where it was, I'd never been to Poland before, I didn't speak a word of Polish, nobody had come to pick me up or anything, all I had was this museum's address. I got a taxi, and the taxi driver seemed very nice but he didn't speak a word of English. He took me to this strange building with wrought iron gates, I didn't think it was a museum at all and everywhere was dark, there was no light on in the place. The taxi driver looked at me and sort of nodded that this was it and I paid him, he'd got a meter so I knew how many złotys to pay him and I gave him a tip, which was a great thing to do as it turned out.

I got out and I couldn't find a bell, just this wrought iron fence. I walked up and down this place, it took about five minutes for me to walk the length of one side and when I came back he was still there. He got out of his taxi and we walked the length of the other side because it was on a corner, but still there was nothing so he went back the side I'd gone first and by that time a huge Alsatian appeared behind the fence barking like mad. I was lost without this man, he was wonderful like taxi drivers can be, it's not the first time I've had a really good taxi driver. He managed to find a bell and after about five minutes of ringing it a sleepy night watchman/caretaker came out and grabbed hold of the Alsatian (which I found out in the end was quite tame because I had to go past this thing all the time I stayed there) and let me in.

It was quite obvious he knew nothing about me coming. The taxi driver went off, I didn't even have the language to thank him, I shook his hand and then the caretaker took me in his little hut because it was freezing and started ringing people up. In the end Anna Saciuk-Gasowska, who curated along with Pauline, arrived and showed me where I was going to be staying.

We weren't actually in the Museum of Modern Art, we were in a museum but I was never quite sure of what the museum was about, I think it had been the house of one of the mill owners and some other museum had taken it over, and this was where I was staying. She led me up to a really nice room where I was going to stay, like a hotel room, with a little en suite shower. She spoke perfect English and of course I was a bit hungry so I said, 'is there anywhere I can get any food?' It was completely black outside, there were hardly any street lamps, and she said 'well I've got to go home now' because she'd obviously got a family, so she pointed me across the road, told the caretaker I was going to buy some food and off I went.

I got into this shop and it was like being in the 1940s, it was just full of tins, there was nothing else but tins, there wasn't even a loaf of bread, just tinned everything. And the only thing I recognised was tinned sardines, or what I thought were sardines, so I bought that. I didn't know any Polish and the woman just took the money, whatever she wanted for the tin of sardines, I'm sure she didn't cheat me but I hadn't got a clue.

I walked back to the museum and I thought, well all I've got is these sardines, and then I realised I'd got no fork. I'd travelled light, I'd got one pair of black trousers and I'd got several shirts and underpants and socks, you know, because they're the things you get through, but I'd only got one pair of trousers. You know how those sardine tins work, you peel back the top, and the oil went all over my trousers because I was sitting on the bed as the room didn't have a chair. You can imagine the fishy smelling oil, and I was supposed to meet these museum people in the morning.

It's about midnight by now and I'm tired and I'm angry and I'm upset and then I looked around this flat and I managed to find what I think must have been liquid soap. The great thing, the saving of my life, was that because it was 18° below zero they had these big old-fashioned radiators which were absolutely boiling. So I then proceeded to wash my trousers, knowing, because Anna had already told me, that the Director of the Museum of Modern Art was in the room next door to me, so I washed my trousers out, shoved them on the radiator just praying that in the morning they would be presentable, and went to bed.

When I got up in the morning and went over to the radiator my trousers were perfectly dry but they still had a slightly fishy smell to them. Anna came and took me off to the Museum of Modern Art which was quite a long way, a good half an hour's drive from where I was staying, and I had no idea where I was. I didn't have a map and I was rather stupid really not to ask Anna for a map. She introduced me to the people at the museum, Pauline Kirk, who was the first person to get in touch with me, and then a chap who was an art historian. They made me very welcome and they took me downstairs into the basement and showed me my piece of sculpture. It was a folded up aluminium piece which was painted with acrylic paint and exhibited at the Grabowski Gallery in 1966-67 after I left St Martin's. Grabowski had bought this piece off me and that's how it ended up in Łódź Museum because when he died he gave his collection to the Łódź Museum, which included my piece, a piece by Bridget Riley and a piece by John Hoyland, people like that, so I was with really well known people. I knew both artists, not directly but indirectly because my first wife worked for Bridget Riley, and I knew John Hoyland because he both taught me and we met up again after I left St Martin's.

The museum people introduced me to the people that were going to restore my piece. Now you're looking at something which was painted at the time when acrylic paint had just come out, I think it was called Cryla in those days. It was green, red and blue and it was badly scratched, and I was thinking, 'well how are they going to restore this? Perhaps what I should do is just take it back home, sand it all down and respray it completely'. I was very very worried about it because I thought 'I don't want it looking bad on exhibition. How did it get scratched so badly?'

What I didn't know was it had been exhibited in Poland for some time. It had gone off to an exhibition at Gdansk and nobody had informed me because they didn't know who I was. It had been going round exhibitions in Poland as the Grabowski Collection, until or even after he'd given it to the Łódź Museum of Modern Art.

So I said to Anna that I should I take it home, and she said 'no no they'll do it, it'll be fine, don't worry about it' so I thought, 'don't worry about it, you're here, you've never been here before, just make the most of it'.

She started taking me round, showing me the factories, showing me where the new Museum of Modern Art would be, which was in this huge factory complex called Manufaktura. It was about two or three factories, like a big square with these big factories coming off, which was going to be (and now is) like a huge shopping precinct, but was also going to have a museum in one of the buildings. Then she drove me back to the museum where I was staying and sort of left me to my own devices.

The day was still young, it was the afternoon, so I thought I'd start to wander around. It was freezing cold, there was snow everywhere and ice so she'd already pointed me in the direction of a restaurant and I thought 'I'm hungry, it's midday' and I passed a restaurant which was just off one of these huge complexes that I told you about which was built for the workers. It looked like a really nice warm restaurant from the outside, so I went in and of course the whole menu was in Polish. The waitress, who seemed a very nice young lady, didn't speak any English and the other daunting thing was there was nobody else in the restaurant but me. I didn't know when they closed and when they opened, but anyway I thought 'well you're just going to have to order'. There were three courses, starter, main meal and pudding, I just had to go for it. I had some fish and it was very nice, it's a river fish, I don't think it was carp but they have it quite a lot out there, I can't remember what it was but I had this fish again and again while I was there. I didn't quite understand what the starter was. The meal was fine, I ordered some wine, of course they're big vodka drinkers but their wines are not too bad.

I had a good meal and I felt really good. I've always been good at walking round cities and finding my way even without a map but most of the time I'm reliant on where the sun is to know which direction I'm going in and of course it was cloudy. There was snow everywhere, but it wasn't yet snowing again and I thought, well, all I've got to do is just make a mental note of which direction I go in and then reverse it. I managed to get back and find the museum about 9 o'clock at night and I thought, 'never again, I'm going to take the address with me in future so I can always get a taxi back'.

The following day Anna took me out and that was a good day, because we visited the art school in Łódź , I was introduced to the people that ran it. It was a beautiful art school in a huge modern building, quite academically taught. Then they took me off to the thing I really wanted to see which was the Łódź Film School where Kieślowski and Wajda and everybody came from, and that was really interesting for me. I saw these old cameras that Wajda had made to make *Man of Iron*, and the old films and things, and I met some interesting people.

Then of course I started to want to know more about Łódź , so I asked Anna, and she gave me a map that showed me where the Jewish cemetery was so I decided to go and see that. I made my way to the Jewish Cemetery and I didn't know at that time that it was in the area of what was the Ghetto. Funnily enough, it's how coincidences go isn't it, as soon as I came back from Łódź somebody lent me a book on the Ghetto in Łódź , about this Rumkowski character who ran the ghetto for the Nazis, he was Jewish, and it's a very sad story.

When I got to the cemetery it was all locked up and it said, 'if you want to get into the cemetery ring this number'. Well I tried ringing it and I couldn't get anywhere, partly because I expected the person on the other end to speak Polish, it appears they don't, they actually speak English. I know people who've got into the cemetery, but I never did. I noticed anti-Semitic graffiti, new anti-Semitic graffiti and I thought 'what's going on here?' but once I'd got a better understanding of Poland I realised that it is like England, you've got your educated people who are not at all racist I don't think as far as I could tell by talking to them, but then you've got a poverty class, and you've got a very peasant-orientated class. Some of the fields were still being ploughed by horses and cows and things, even now, so there were a lot of different elements some of which are not very nice.

Once I got out in the countryside, it was more obvious that it is incredibly poor. Kieślowski made three films called *Red*, *White* and *Blue*, and *White* is a really funny story about this man who wants to get back to Poland and at one point he's out in the countryside and it really does show you what a lot of Poland's like, although Poland's very varied. A lot of the parts that I was near are very flat and almost fenland-like, but if you go towards Lublin they get very hilly and it's much more forested so it's very different, and Kraków is different again.

So I never got into the Jewish cemetery but later I found out a lot about the history of the Jewish Polish people and how like a lot of other European countries the borders of Poland have always moved. The Sudetenland was where the German Poles lived so you've got a lot of different interactions of people, some people had sided with Hitler just like the Vichy government in France, so you'd got a lot of collusion, and some parts colluding with the Russians when the Russians came in, so you've got a lot of mixed feelings about what went on during and after the war.

One of the films I saw just after I came back from Łódź the second time, about a year later, was *Katyn* which was made by Wajda, who must have been in his 80s when he made it, and it was the story of his father. I didn't know that his father was an officer in the Polish army and the Russians had got them and killed off 20,000 officers by shooting them in pits and his father was one, and then they blamed it onto the Germans, it only came out recently, and in fact it took the Russians only till recently to actually apologise and it was a very strange apology, really.

Łódź was a very strange place when I went out there, it's obviously improved now but when I first went there was a lot of waste land with bonfires going with men drinking vodka out of bottles. It was very derelict and there were obviously a lot of people out of work. It was poor, and it's a poor place, it was much poorer than Warsaw or Kraków obviously because everything had been channelled for a hundred years into the textile industry and when that had gone it just collapsed in on itself, whereas Warsaw and Kraków were much more cosmopolitan, they'd got more varied industries.

But there was a lot of interest for me to go there because it's one of those things where I didn't know I was going there and then it opened up all sorts of things. I saw the connection for a start, more of a realisation than I ever imagined, between my art and the 20th century art in Eastern Europe. I always knew when I was at St Martin's that I was influenced by the Russian Constructivists, the ideas that came out of a new sort of abstract art that was supposed to relate to everybody, but I didn't realise that it had spread so far. I knew of the Russian Constructivists, I knew of the Bauhaus, but I didn't know about the art of all these intermediary Eastern Bloc countries like Hungary and Poland so that was a real eye-opener, and to see the connection between me and Kobro's work, because there is a connection there, not in the sense that I was influenced by her work, I think I only knew of one piece, but just in the way that she had developed the same understanding of abstraction and bending metal like I'd done. So that was of real interest to me.

At the same time, it was quite interesting to find out the history of this place and the sort of anthropological way that things had developed - the reasons why there was Modernism there, because they were an industrial city like Barcelona with Art Noucentisme, they were a rich industrial area before the war so they could afford to expand within their cultural means of film and sculpture and art and culture so that they'd embraced everything that Russia and Germany had embraced but in a Polish way.

163

A year later I was invited to the private view of the exhibition that Anna had curated called *The Swinging Sixties in London* and as I've said before, Grabowski was one of only two or three contemporary exhibition spaces in London at the time so it was quite an interesting exhibition to see what was going on, with pieces from people like Derek Boshier, Bridget Riley and John Hoyland. It was amazing because the minute I got there - I didn't stay in the place I'd stayed in before, I think they put me up in a hotel - the museum itself was dusty looking and you could tell they were waiting to move into the new place. I was interested in the art work but the museum was just falling to pieces, in fact everything inside and out was falling to pieces, the whole of Łódź was falling to pieces except for this big place Manufaktura, which was going to be the big shopping precinct. There was another shopping precinct which was brand new actually and that was some distance from Manufaktura down the main street of Łódź , which was quite an interesting street and off there was a Russian orthodox church all made out of wood. There were lots of interesting buildings although they're falling to pieces.

So I was back in the Museum of Modern Art, saw my piece that was on show, and I was absolutely mesmerised by it because they'd done a fantastic job, I couldn't see where they'd retouched it at all, and it was exactly the same colour as it had been when I first made it. I said to Anna 'they haven't resprayed the whole thing have they?' and she said, 'no we couldn't possibly do that. It's all scientifically done now'. We went to see the women who did the restoration and I saw some of the stuff that they'd made. It was incredible how they do it, they analyse what was in the paint and then they mix it up again and make it. So it was fantastic and the private view was quite interesting because there were very few of us who'd come from those days, Frank Dolphin and Susan Swale, who were present at the private view. But anyway, the private view took place and I made sure I took two pairs of trousers this time, I always make sure I take two pairs of trousers now everywhere I go and the new director was there, a very nice young man, and then suddenly in the middle of the private view, there's flashlights going off, and there's about 200 people there and then Anna said 'now Douglas Jeal will talk about his work' and it wasn't the first time that it had happened to me but I was put on the spot because I didn't know it was going to happen and I just rambled on about Grabowski which was a good thing to do because Grabowski's son was there and I believe I've mentioned before to you that the whole reason he got into art was because his other son was an artist and he'd died. So I met his son, who I've been in touch with since, who lives in Wimbledon in London, and it was a very well attended private view and I got to know Łódź much better.

I was invited to go and see the Grabowski Museum. As I said before, the place that he had in the 1960s in Sloane Avenue, the back half was a chemist's, the front was the gallery. He'd also got this museum of pharmacy in Kraków and it is a most amazing museum to go to because there is the history of chemistry. I met the Director - I think she's the Director - at the Museum of Modern Art opening and she invited me to go and see it and said she would show me round which she did do, she was a very nice lady, and it was fantastic, an incredible little museum. The museum itself is I think in an old pharmacy but it's a very very beautiful building and Kraków is much older, the buildings are much older whereas Łódź is 1930s.

And before I went there I went off to Warsaw. The trouble with Warsaw, because of what happened to Warsaw it's a very strange feeling because it's all been rebuilt, so at the moment all these reconstructed old buildings still look a bit like a theatre set. It's the same with parts of Kraków too, some places have been rebuilt and you get that feeling that they look old but they're not old, you're very aware of that, so it looks like a theatre set. But Kraków was quite an interesting place and I got some good photos. I was quite mesmerised by the trams and things like that, I get into all sorts of different things. I mean I do like to go to museums of modern art and so on, but I also like parks and things and I get fascinated by seeing how cities have come together and worked themselves out, so I was rather impressed with Kraków .

Warsaw I did like and there are parts of Warsaw on the outskirts which is like Łódź where the Soviets have built these huge blocks of flats for the workers, but having said that they're nothing like we built in the 1960s, they're not tall horrible buildings, they're quite elongated with probably three or four floors at the most. They're very much better set out, they're more like a Le Corbusier way of setting things out than our awful hodge-podge of the 1960s. What they've done is paint them really nice colours on the outside and they're not bad. I mean, I don't know what they're like to live in, the people seem quite friendly.

I took the train from Łódź to Kraków and again that was quite interesting because it took virtually the same route that the Jews would have taken, you go up north and then you come back south. So that wasn't too nice because I didn't realise it at first and then I thought, knowing where the sun was, this was the summer the second time I went, and knowing where the sun was I thought 'why are we going north?' because that's the way the train tracks go and that's the way that they would have gone. By that time I'd read about what happened to them, and some of the stations we stopped at were where they would have got off when they were taken to concentration camps.

Łódź, Warsaw and Kraków, they're the main places, and Gdansk, but I never got to Gdansk, although like I said I think my piece had been exhibited there. So all in all that was quite a nice experience to go there and to be shown around, lots of people wanted to know what sort of new work I was doing and I went off to see one of the factories that was beginning to be turned into a community arts centre and it was fantastic, it was just everything we want over here in England, beautiful, you're talking about on the size of at least the turbine hall in the Tate Modern. These buildings are huge because they housed all the textile machines, they're all empty, there's no walls inside, there's just cast iron pillars to hold up the next floor and then they've got big windows so they let in a lot of light so they're very very beautiful buildings. I even thought at the time, could I afford to buy one of these buildings, because especially the first time I was out there you got the impression that things were very very cheap and most people were renting. And the second time I went out there was for the private view and the exhibition and that went well and then I was invited the following year to go to a symposium in Lublin.

When I got back from Łódź the first time I'd gone back to work on the *Codex*. As I said, I was gathering together images about all these things that were important to me in the 20th century. Some of them were nice images, I used a beautiful photograph of a pregnant woman and a really nice image of a foetus in a womb, but unfortunately most of it when I looked at the 20th century was pretty horrendous.

When I made *Famine* in the 1970s, I'd collected material for it and I'd paid for some photographs from Save the Children which were originally done by Mike Wells, a very well known photographer who went out to Africa and photographed the famine out there. I started by using some of the images from that to put on the *Codex*. I used other images of photographs that I like for one reason or another, there were some photographs by Dorothea Lange of the prospectors going out in the West of America in the 1930s.

I got some extraordinary photos from a book I read about the Łódź ghetto. The ghetto in Łódź was divided into two, and between it the Nazis had constructed a wooden bridge because there was a main thoroughfare and they didn't want the Jews to mix with the Germans or the Poles. I had an amazing photograph of the Jews with their Stars of David crossing the bridge every morning to go to work. So I started to superimpose these images on the acrylic shapes that I was making for the *Codex*.

I made about 48 separate pieces which gave me about 24 linked pairs and I hung them in a row and I was thinking about where to exhibit them. From going to Łódź I'd been invited to a symposium being organised by the museum of Lublin. They wanted me to give a talk and for them to have one of my pieces, so I thought, what better piece to talk about and give them than the *Codex*.

Lublin was completely different from Łódź . It was a symposium on abstract art and there were Polish people and people from all over the world, including a German painter, Dirk Rathke, who I've got very friendly with who lives in Berlin and I went to visit him later in Berlin.

The symposium was held in a beautiful old castle in the mountains, right up high overlooking the most beautiful countryside, and we were put up in an old manor with a five minute walk to the castle. We were there for four or five days, miles away from anywhere so we couldn't get anything, everything was provided for us, the food was fantastic, the drink was provided, mostly vodka. Dirk and I and a couple of other Germans that I got very friendly with did manage to go down to the local village and buy a bottle of wine as something different from the vodka.

If you can imagine a group of predominantly male artists, there were some females but predominantly male, who all drank, in this beautiful setting miles from anywhere. It wasn't a drunken orgy, it was just a lot of intense talking, like symposiums are, but with a lot of alcohol and being completely isolated. Even to get to the nearest village you had to get into a car and drive. But it was very beautiful and we went on a couple of walks, and it was really lovely.

We all gave presentations and talked about our work, and I talked about the *Codex*, which went down really well. It fitted in really nicely because I didn't know I was going to be invited when I'd started work on it, it was another amazing coincidence.

Then the Museum of Lublin acquired *Codex* off me and they've got it as part of their collection now. I don't know if it's been shown, the problem with the Polish museums like I found out with the original 1960s piece, it had been shown many times, in Gdansk and all over Poland and I'd never heard about it, so I don't know how many times the *Codex* has been shown.

That was my third time in Poland and then I had a fourth time which Anna arranged where I rented the studio of a painter in Łódź and that was a good time for me too, I enjoyed that because I had a flat to myself. That's when I really got to know Łódź because I was in Łódź for about a month to six weeks and I went out and bought my food, I began to pick up words of Polish and really did enjoy being there. I didn't really meet anybody that time, I think Anna was away. I used to go drawing in a park next to the flat. I couldn't make sculpture but I was painting most of the time, although I didn't like a lot of the paintings I did, I don't know whether it was the light or what. When I had to come back I thought 'I don't want to take these canvases' so some of them I painted over and left to the person whose flat it was and some I gave to Anna, I think Anna's got two or three of my paintings. I think I made some little maquettes as well, she may have one of those.

That was the last time I was there, and it was quite good because I suppose what I was doing was putting all my thoughts together, you know how you put all your thoughts together for a change, and I haven't been back since. Then I started to go to Berlin, partly to see Dirk and also because, while I'd been to Germany in the 1970s, to Cologne and Hamburg for exhibitions and things, I'd never been to Berlin. So I was sort of thinking about going to Berlin and what that was going to be like, and that for the present is the end of the phase of the Łódź episode, which was quite eventful I think and it hasn't gone from my memory completely yet. I think there are always things that are left in your subconscious that are unsaid, that obviously happened when you think I went to Mexico in 1994 and it wasn't until 2007/8 that I started making the *Codices*. All that time it had been up there in my subconscious but hadn't come out and I was formulating different ideas.

Chapter 17 - The Dancer and the Accident 2008-2010

That whole period after my divorce and Angie leaving home, and then travelling to Poland, was quite a fruitful time in lots of ways, but unfortunately I lost the studio I had at the university (which by now had changed again from APU to Anglia Ruskin) because they moved the sculpture department from the annexe where it was and back into the main building. I knew then that I had to make a studio at home, so I changed the garage into a workshop, insulated the attic and put a floor in it and everything so that I could store a lot of my work up there, moved into a smaller bedroom, and started using the big front bedroom as a construction studio.

In about 2008 I was invited to sit on the Public Art Steering Group for Cambridge City Council. I'd been interested in working with the council for a long time. When I first went to Barcelona I'd met the people who were doing the new parks and incorporating a lot of sculpture. If you drive through France and Spain, at every lay-by along the motorways, they have this little pull-in where you can just have a picnic and they all have big pieces of sculpture. I was amazed by all this and when I came back I found out the same was going on at Glasgow School of Art, they had this special relationship with the council where the council were giving them temporary and permanent space. So when I started being involved with the city council I suggested to them that they give students studio space, first of all David Ryan and I managed to negotiate with the council and at that time we were given mostly old industrial sites that they couldn't rent out and we were given them for a period of a week or two weeks, so we had exhibitions with the students, just the students.

And then Elaine Midgely from the council took it up, she is a very enthusiastic person and has been very helpful. She was then at the Junction running the leisure things, I can't remember her exact title. A lot of spaces in empty shops had become available because of the economic crisis, and she set up spaces for artists in these shops. There are about four or five shops altogether in Cambridge at this very moment that are showing art, again it's a one-off thing for a week or two, whatever they've got it for. A very good ex-student of mine, Angie Jackson-Maine, has been very prominent in this, and she's really put everything in and helped other students to get their work shown, and so that's been made available to us.

All in all I suppose I'm a happy person and a positive person, but when I lost my studio that was a big headache to me because that was a nice, big studio and it was that time, I really did think, perhaps I ought to move out of the country and find somewhere where I can work. I went to see Dirk in Berlin and when I came back I was very undecided. One of the things I didn't like about it was that everybody seemed to be moving to Berlin, it seemed to be the new craze, like Picasso going to Paris, it was the craze to go to Berlin, so I didn't like that in a way, but I did like Dirk's studio, which was a really nice studio in an old 19th century factory building. They weren't pulling down their 19th century small craftsmen factories like they did in Barcelona, which is a shame because those are the very places that artists generally go for renting, old factory space or industrial space. Things were cheaper in Berlin, and I did have to think twice about it, but the other thing that I didn't like, like in Poland, was the weather.

Poland was another place that was fairly cheap, and as I said I did actually rent a place out there in Łódź for a while. I rather liked Łódź because it was a big old industrial city with a lot of really nice old 19th century industrial buildings, and unpretentious, but what I couldn't take when I first arrived there was the cold. It gets bitter there, 15-19° below zero with a wind most probably from Siberia. It's a dry cold which is quite nice in a way, you don't notice it so much as England's cold which is a damp cold, you can actually dress up and go out in it, but I thought no, if I'm going to move I'd rather move to somewhere where it's a warmer climate.

One advantage I suppose of being on your own in the evenings is I've read a lot. I always did read, but I have read an incredible amount in the last ten years, anything from philosophy to novels, lots of people's biographies, Epstein, Giacometti and many more, and I've carried on my interest in poetry. I've gone to see a lot of contemporary dance, I've always had this fondness for dance, I used Stravinsky's *Rite of Spring* in the 1960s to make my big final-year piece of sculpture at St Martin's, and my ex-wife's sister was a contemporary dance choreographer who used to dance regularly at The Place in London. Angie and I first saw Siobhan Davies Dance at the Arts Theatre in Cambridge, they used to coming to Cambridge regularly each year, and I would go and see them whenever they came.

I'd always wanted to do theatre and costume, not in the same way as Picasso and Diaghilev, I wanted it to be more sculpture-orientated rather than just doing costumes, so I started thinking more about that. One of the biggest problems I suppose I've always had is what the Buddhists call monkey-mind, where you get too many ideas and I often have to really restrict myself. Sometimes the material does that for me, I've found, which is good. Because I can paint, I sculpt, I write poetry, I write a dialogue about things I've seen, I draw quite regularly. I've had periods when I've drawn much more than I do at the moment, in the 1970s I did lots and lots of drawings, I sometimes still do drawing for ideas and I like sitting in parks and drawing the space between me and people and trees and things. When I lived in Farm Cottage if I got bored making sculpture I went out and did a lot of tree drawings. I am quite fascinated by trees, it has something to do with the discipline I got from reading Zen when I was in my twenties and I wanted to be able to draw trees exactly and to show the structure of them and the way that they're worked out, because all trees are different.

All in all I think that the monkey-mind doesn't often do me any good because I'm just pulled in too many directions and that happens very regularly. I think I've learned to cope with that and say to myself 'no, put that off till you've finished what you're doing' and in some ways that may be a good thing because that gives ideas a chance to mature properly. I think that's what happened with a lot of my best ideas like *Famine*, *Shelter*, the *Codices*, *Escrito de Campo* and things like that. I think they had time to mature because I was doing other things and had to put them off.

When I first moved up to Cambridgeshire with my first wife we lived at St Ives near the river in Bridge Street, and I've always liked St Ives, I've always like being near the river. I remember when I was living with my grandmother as a child she used to take me to a little river at Beddington near Croydon, we got there by bus and I played in the water in the little stream. So I've always had this thing with water, and I started doing some water drawings when I was living at St Ives in the 1970s, and in about 2009, 2010 I started going back there and setting off walking either from Houghton or Hemingford Abbotts, finding trees and drawing them. Some of them are pen and ink and some are pencil, quite quick drawings, some are good, not all of them.

One winter day I was there drawing some trees in the freezing cold, I was wrapped up but after about an hour or so, you don't realise it but you're getting really stiff, you get up and you can't bend your knees, it's a really weird sensation, you're almost like frozen, I've done this before. On this occasion I got up from doing one particular drawing, and I was quite excited – I don't know why because when I look at it now it's not very good – but I was quite excited so I danced down this lane, sort of half running half dancing. I often get excited because I go and do a drawing and I come back and make a piece of sculpture, not necessarily of the drawing but I'm always doing something.

And I was quite excited, so of course I fell over, and I really went with a bang, I fell over on my right side, it was rather embarrassing really because it had just begun to thaw so the whole of my right side had mud on it and I'd got about three miles to walk back to the car along this footpath with everybody looking at me. Luckily there weren't that many people out because it was so cold, but I got up and I thought 'well I'm all right really'. I was quite shocked because I really did go over but I walked back to the car and drove home. The next day I didn't feel so good and I went off to see the doctor and had an x-ray on my hip and they said 'we can't see anything'. I had a strange pain in the groin that lasted about 3 months, and I told the doctor but she said, 'oh it's just muscle', so I didn't think any more of it.

Then a bit later in 2010 I started getting a rash. I've always had allergies, from when I was a child, I came out like a lobster and the doctor sent me to the St John's skin hospital in London where they found out that I was allergic to artificial fibres, and my mother would buy me nylon underpants. So since then I've always had to wear cotton. When it started up again, the doctor said 'well, there's no point trying to find out what it is, you've got very sensitive skin anyway, you can't wear artificial fibres. It could be anything, you could go through all the foodstuffs, but it could take maybe ten years to find out what it is' she said 'if it gets really bad we'll send you back to St John's skin hospital, but it's not really that bad, if you take these pills it'll go away'.

I took the pills and it did go away, but one of the things the doctor said it could be is dust. Well my workshop is full of dust. Angie was always complaining because there were spider webs, especially as I have a lot of plants, I do actually clean the spider webs down, but what with the plants it's a never-ending task, because plants attract spiders.

So I went out and bought a new Dyson vacuum cleaner, and I was enthralled with the packaging. As a sculptor I've always liked playing with materials, so I started playing with the cardboard, and I made a life-sized cardboard figure and then put photocopies on it. The photocopies came from when I did *Inside Out* in Barcelona, the sculpture which was about Fellini's *Eight and a Half*, the film about making a film. As I've said before, I took photographs of the sculpture as I made it and then I got really interested in photography and I started superimposing some negatives on other negatives and I rather liked all these abstract shapes that I was coming out with in the photographs. So then I took them and photocopied them and I photocopied some onto transparencies and put photographs of itself onto the piece.

When I was making the cardboard figure I still had all the photocopy tryouts and I rather liked the shape so when I'd made this thing in cardboard I pasted on all these photocopies. Because of my interest in dance, I made it to represent a dancer standing with her hands behind her back resting on the barre. When I'd finished it I thought, well, it's cardboard, it's not going to last very long, and I was just starting to think about making something a bit more robust.

This was towards the end of 2010. I was expecting to retire from teaching the following year, and I'd just met Linda Hadfield at a private view of an exhibition by one of my ex-students, Susi Gutierrez. Linda had created a website for Susi, and I was thinking I needed a website as a showcase for my work so that I could sell more of my pieces and generate some income after I retired. So Linda and I met a couple of times to discuss her making me one.

Then in November 2010 I had another fall, and this one was much more serious than the first. I was shopping in Sainsbury's, going to get a loaf of bread, and I slipped on some grapes that were on the floor and I went with quite a bang. I'd never really had a bad accident before, I broke my wrist in Barcelona but then I just got up and went off to hospital. But when you're lying on the floor and you can't move and these first aiders from Sainsbury's are saying: 'see if you can stand up', well I knew I couldn't stand up I was in so much pain. I couldn't move my leg at all, it was doubled up but the pressure was forcing it down, every time it forced it down I was literally screaming with pain. A man who was shopping stopped and he held it up for me, for about 20 minutes he held my leg in place. Another shopper, a woman who was most probably an East European took her overcoat off and put it under my head. The first aiders, three of them from Sainsbury's just stood there and watched all this, and bungled it because one thought the other or the desk had rung for the ambulance, but they hadn't, so instead of taking about 10 minutes, because this Sainsbury's is only about 10 minutes from the hospital, it took me about half an hour to get to hospital.

They gave me a load of morphine in the ambulance because they realised I was in a lot of pain and when I got to the A&E there was a really nice man who obviously knew what he was doing. They took me to x-ray first, they x-rayed it and said 'you've fractured the top of your femur in several places' and he said 'I'm going to have to straighten it out. You won't believe this but it starts setting straight away' he said 'I've got to straighten it out'. He gave me another shot of morphine and he got hold of my leg and yanked it, he knew what he was doing but I just went through the roof with the pain and then they took me and put me in traction.

It was then that I realised I'd done the same injury as a friend called Colin Poynter when I was at Croydon School of Art. Colin Poynter did graphics, most of the boys who came from working class backgrounds did graphics, it was only me and Frank Carver who did fine arts, and Colin had a motor bike and he came off it. The surgeon said that what I'd done was like a

174

classic motor bike accident, it was the sort of fracture which you get coming off a motor bike. It reminded me when they put me in traction of going to see Colin in hospital and the way they dealt with a fracture of the femur in those days, because they didn't mind how long you stayed in hospital in those days, you stayed in hospital and then you went convalescent, and Colin spent six months with his leg in traction. Every time I went to see him he complained about the bed pan and the sores on his backside because they weren't allowed to move, they were actually in bed for six months in those days, and so obviously there's been a revolution in medicine since then, nowadays they pin it for you which is what they've done for me, I've now got a stainless steel pin in my leg.

I wasn't feeling depressed then because I'd got all this morphine in me and I remember, when I went into hospital it was quite mild, but the weather changed and people kept coming in to see me and saying 'it's freezing out there'. I was in a ward where I had a lovely view of the Magog Hills so I used to look out the window and it took me back to my school days, when I was forever looking out the window, I used to just switch off and look out the window and watch the clouds, like you do when you're a child, and that's what I did so I was relatively happy. I tried to read, people brought me books and I tried to read in hospital but I don't know why I just didn't feel like reading. Then I asked for a sketch book and a pencil and I thought I'd do loads of drawings but I didn't do that either.

I did one of a man opposite, and he was a strange sort of personality, he'd got some funny views, you know the sort of views you meet from the *Sun* newspaper, but I was absolutely entranced by this man. He had had a hip operation, and the difference between a hip operation and smashing up your femur is that they get you up on your feet with a hip operation as soon as you've done it whereas I couldn't put any weight on my right leg, I couldn't put my right leg down on the ground for three months. You mustn't put any pressure on it, you have to just put your big toe on the ground when you walk with the crutches, so that when your leg mends it mends in a straight line rather than to one side or the other, so you have to just touch the toe but you mustn't put any pressure on.

But this other chap was up straight away, so I saw his body, and I kept thinking 'where have I seen that body before?' and then I remembered it was the drawings I'd done of Guy the gorilla at London Zoo and he just looked like Guy the gorilla, I couldn't get over it, so I thought, I must do a drawing of it, so I did a drawing of him in bed, but other than that I didn't really feel like drawing very much.

I think it was the morphine. The morphine was making me think about my life, not in a bad way. The surgeon had actually said to me: 'It's all gone okay. You won't be able to put your foot down for three months, you'll be on two crutches for at least three months, you won't be able to get upstairs, you'll be on a single crutch for six months' in other words he said to me 'it'll take you eighteen months to get back to anything like you were before you had the accident' and I thought, 'no I'm not having that!' but I didn't know what the future held, I didn't know what chaos it would be.

People came to see me, my daughter came to see me and when I knew I was coming out I asked her and her partner to put me a bed downstairs in the living room. I was in for two weeks because they wouldn't let me out without anybody looking after me. Everybody was so good to me in the hospital, from the minute the ambulance picked me up - I know people criticise hospital workers but I was amazed by them. I was amazed by the ward, there were only two or three nurses, they'd got two or three wards to look after, they were on the go all night, people were ringing the bells for them all the time - 'can I have a bottle, can I do this' and I was amazed by it all. I've got no criticism, absolutely no criticism at all of them, and the physiotherapy people and the welfare people at Addenbrookes Hospital they certainly weren't going to let me out on my own, I couldn't have coped. So they got everything in place for me.

The ambulance was supposed to come at twelve o'clock in the afternoon, and I was sitting downstairs in the wheelchair, waiting to go and there was still ice on the ground so of course people were falling and doing injuries like mine all the time so there weren't enough ambulances and I had to wait, that's basically it, it wasn't their fault.

I arrived home in the freezing cold at eight o'clock in the evening, they brought me in a wheelchair, the two people in the ambulance got me into bed, the heating wasn't on, it was freezing cold, and I think one of the ambulance people got me a blanket because he was frightened I was going to be cold and he said 'there will be somebody with you either tonight or tomorrow' and of course they had to go. I can't remember how it happened, I think they had to leave the door open, but anyway within half an hour this woman came, the social worker – I'm not sure what she was but she was there to sort out my care, she came to go over what I needed and she said 'this is impossible you need complete care' so she got on the phone and arranged it and she said 'why isn't there any heating on? Can you call up somebody to get your heating on?' So I called my friend Tony and he came the following day and each time someone knocked at the door I would have had to get up so I got this woman to put the key under a stone so people called me on the phone and I told them where the key was so I didn't have to get up.

She organised three daily helps for me, I got breakfast, lunch and dinner and they came and washed me, in bed, they had to do a bed bath or whatever it's called. I could get to the bathroom to go to the toilet though, because they wouldn't let me out of hospital until I could use a zimmer frame, that was one of the criteria to let me go home.

I'd got these ladies coming and they were really helpful and lovely. I didn't know who was coming, they changed, I had about five or six different women over the period of time but they were really great to me.

Tony came to see me the day after I came out and he said 'you can't exist like this, it's freezing in here' he tried to get the heating on and he said 'I'm going to get a friend to come and look at the heating for you'. He was good intentioned and so was the friend but he was an absolute disaster really, I don't think he really knew what he was doing.

He spent a whole day here while I was in bed. And he said: 'I've got it working, it's fine now but if you get any problems just give me a ring'. Anyway about 3 o'clock in the morning I woke up and I could hear water dripping so I thought, 'Bloody hell, what am I going to do? I've got to get up', so I got up with the zimmer frame and the whole of the back wall, on the ceiling, was dripping with water. There was absolutely nothing I could do, I couldn't get upstairs to see what had happened, I couldn't do anything. So in the morning I called up Tony and this bloke, and what he'd done, he'd forgotten to do up the two radiator valves so they were leaking.

There was still no heat downstairs, though there was heat upstairs, so they told me, but he spent another day here and reckoned he'd got it done. I was frozen all the next day, and of course the people that came in were having a go at me they said 'you can't have this'. Paul came round, he was a colleague from APU, an art historian who'd retired earlier, and he lives in Sawston, and he brought me an electric fire, so I had an electric fire going all the time.

This bloke had disappeared and said he'd done it, then luckily Richard, my friend who lives in France, came over and he arrived and said 'nothing's happening'. He went upstairs and he said 'all the hot water is going from the heater into the header tank in the attic and it's like a tropical forest up there. The water is just dripping off the roof, and all your work's getting damaged'.

Richard phoned this bloke up and told him to get lost, basically, and he got British Gas here. And it was fantastic because there was this Irishman, I can't remember his name, but he was such a character, and I was in bed, Richard sat there and this Irish bloke sat here and he said: 'You're completely disabled' he said 'we're not having that! I promise that I will get it done by tomorrow, it will be all finished by tomorrow' and Richard and I looked at each other. I'd been like that for about a week by then.

Anyway, lo and behold, he'd got all the doors open, it was still freezing cold out there, but the Irish bloke got two teams of blokes here, and they did it in a day, they put in all the new radiators, a new boiler, everything, they got it done in a single day, which is fantastic really. It cost me four and a half thousand pounds, but there was nothing I could do about that. It's just one of those freaks that the system breaks down when you most want it. But then the place had been empty for two weeks in which time it had got really cold.

So I was stuck here and I read, and I didn't have the morphine, they wouldn't give it to me. When I left hospital, they said, after about four days they take you off morphine and he came round and looked at me and he said 'you're really enjoying this morphine, I'm afraid that I'm going to have to take you off it'. I had a big smile on my face, and then they gave me this substitute. He told me that because it's the biggest bone in your body, it's the most painful bone to break, but when he visited me he said 'I think you should be all right'.

Lots of people came round to see me, friends and students would turn up, and ex-students. Paul came round every single day because he was re-tired, which was marvellous, and he was a really good friend. The three home help women were coming in for I don't know how many months, because I couldn't cook. Paul and Petra, who also lives in Sawston, would get the food in for me - bread and stuff like that, for the women to do, because the women didn't actually prepare food, although I think they must have got microwave stuff for me in the beginning because I had nobody here to get it. But Petra took over quite quickly in cooking for me at least every other day, she used to cook really nice dinners and she or Paul would bring them in little plastic cartons and then the women would heat them up in the microwave for me. And Angie ordered some food in for me from Waitrose.

So that was my sort of existence, and then when I was on two crutches they provided me with a seat for the bath, I couldn't swing my right leg over the side of the bath, so there I was completely naked, and I had to ask one of these women to help me. Of course they had to wash quite a bit of me, I couldn't wash my leg, I couldn't bend to get down, so I got used to them washing me.

One of the fears I had in hospital was that this leg was going to be a bit shorter and that can happen, but he said 'no don't worry'. The other fear I had was that I was going to have a limp, which I've got, some days I do have a bit of a limp, other days I'm fine, some days I can dance to anything, and other days I'm in quite a bit of pain. I don't take pain killers, it's not that bad, it's nothing like it was when it happened. I think the pain threshold now has gone up for me because when you've done something like that, the pain I was in before the ambulance got there was just absolutely ridiculous, so after that, I think my tolerance has gone up.

I looked into suing Sainsbury's for negligence, I did get advice, but they came back to me and said the barrister felt I'd got less than a 40% chance of winning, so they're not going to take it on. I wish Mr Kimberley the solicitor I used in the 1970s was still there but I shouldn't imagine he'd be alive now, if he is he'll be in his nineties, but he was certainly a nice person and I'm sure he would have sorted it out.

Chapter 18 - Recovery and Retirement 2011-2012

It was a slow recovery, as I've said, I had to stay downstairs for the first few months. I couldn't do very much but the physiotherapist was coming and telling me what to do. There was a particular physio who came, she'd unfortunately lost her husband quite recently. I think she was being very protective of me and she said 'on no account must you attempt to go upstairs'. Now the physio at the hospital had said: 'When you feel like it try and attempt to go upstairs' because they actually did get me to go up three stairs in the hospital with two crutches, but they said 'make sure there's somebody behind you to catch you if you fall'.

One ex-student, a Chinese lady, turned up one day and I said 'oh good' because I'm here in the bed and I'm thinking 'I want to get upstairs to that studio and start making things' and I'm still on two crutches, you've got to have two crutches because you mustn't put your foot down, but it's difficult because I found the banister was too high for my arm to take the pressure off my right leg so I had to go up using two crutches. So I got her behind me and I said 'I'm going upstairs' and she was saying 'I don't want to do this' and I said, 'look, just stay behind me, and if I start to fall, just grab hold of me'.

Of course I got nearly to the top, and the top of the stairs turns round and I fell but I fell forward not back, so I'm screaming in pain, and she's saying 'What should I do? Shall I call an ambulance? What shall I do?' and I said 'Just give me time, just give me time'. So I sort of lay there for about 10 to 15 minutes till the pain began to wear off and then the problem was to get me down. She wanted to send for an ambulance, I didn't want to send for an ambulance, so I came down on my bottom, and we got me into bed. Then the physio came round, within about an hour of me doing it, and she went berserk 'I told you not to go up the stairs!' And that's the last time I saw that physio because she wouldn't attend me any more, she sent another person.

But it meant that I had to go to the hospital, see the surgeon, have an x-ray, and he was very good, he just sort of smiled at me and said: 'You're okay, all the x-rays have come back and everything's still in place' and he said - because I was smiling - he said: 'I know what you're smiling about, you're smiling that if you've fallen over and it's all right, you're okay' and that was true, that's exactly what I was thinking. So I think I stayed in bed for a week after that. I didn't want to go back to hospital, but within a week I was getting people to get me upstairs.

While I was at the hospital they did a scan, not just a scan on the bones but on the bone density. I went to see Dr Vince and he said 'I've got something to tell you, you've got osteoporosis, you've got to go and see the woman that's in charge of osteoporosis'. I did that the same day, she was waiting for me, they'd already arranged it but they didn't tell me till I got in there. She said 'your bone density is down and you've probably had it for ten years without knowing it' because they knew that really the amount of damage I'd done to myself from just falling on the floor was a bit severe, and that's why they scanned me and found out about the osteoporosis. She said: 'Hopefully the pills will be of some use, they'll keep it at bay. If we catch it early enough we can reverse it, I don't think we've caught it early enough on you but at least we can keep it at the same level'. That's when Dr Vince said to me 'no bungee jumping, no hang-gliding' and they were very good, because they told me I can walk as much as I want, and swim, they didn't advise me to run, I don't know what it is about running, but they advised me to walk and he said 'just carry on making sculpture'. I suppose the psychological thing is just to get people back to normal, so he actually wanted me to make sculpture just as much as I wanted to, it was the physio who was being awkward, the one at home, not the one at the hospital. I suppose she was just being protective.

Because osteoporosis is so unusual in a man, when they told me about it I asked whether any chemicals or anything that I'd worked with in my career might have anything to do with it, and they said 'we don't know. Most probably it was more likely you being a war baby and not getting enough calcium' because rationing went on till about 1952-53, well I was nine by then. I can remember the dried milk we had and we were only allocated one egg, I don't think I had much calcium going in to me and most probably had quite a lot of lead because the piping was all lead.

It's quite funny that two years before I had the accident they took out my saliva gland in my neck. I had a problem when I was a child, we had this horrible orange juice that was like a powder that you mixed up and it tasted vile, it was almost fizzy, like it had got baking powder in it, and every time I drank it my gland swelled up. My mum took me to the doctors and the doctor said 'it's all right, it will stop with age', so nobody did anything about it, and every time I drank orange juice it used to swell up, even real squeezed orange juice, anything acidic. I didn't take any notice of it because it used to go down again, and then in about 2009-10 it swelled up and wouldn't go down. I went to the doctor and she sent me to the hospital and they x-rayed it and what I'd got, they reckoned it was one of the biggest calcium stones they'd ever seen that had lodged itself actually inside the gland, the gland had grown round this calcium stone, and they said, 'We can't do anything but take it out'. So they took it out, but it's pretty ironic to think that they said it was one of the biggest calcium stones they'd ever seen in a gland when I'm missing the calcium in my bones. Maybe it was all going in my neck! Once they took it out I was okay, I'd just put up with it all my life and I didn't eat many oranges because of it, and since then, I love oranges, and I eat them all the time.

It was while I was invalided after the accident that I started working with Linda on the website, because I couldn't do much else. We'd had one meeting in the office, at Anglia Ruskin, we'd just had a general discussion and had arranged a follow-up meeting at home when the accident happened. I didn't have Linda's number in my mobile, but I did have Susi's, the ex-student who introduced us, so I had to call Susi and ask her to let Linda know that I was in hospital.

In a way it was really good because Linda started to come here every couple of weeks. I was pretty disabled, I don't think I started making sculpture for at least six months maybe longer, before I started work on the acrylic version of the *Dancer* figure. I can't remember making any sculpture for six months, the first half of 2011, apart from maybe three or four small pieces.

I was determined to get back on my feet. I was worried that I was going to be crippled. I remember going to see Dr Vince and him saying that I could put my foot down, on the ground, just gently at first, and then another time I went to see him and he got me to stand up - it was still painful - and he said 'you can drive now if you can smash your foot on the brake pedal, but only drive if you're very confident that you can drive' and I was, I was confident and I did it. The only problem I had with driving was getting in and out of the car, and that hurt me more than actually driving.

As soon as I could drive I went over to St Ives, taking my crutches because I still needed them. I remember thinking to myself 'How far?' because I often walk from St Ives to Houghton and over the mill, and that's about four to six miles round trip, and I remember thinking 'How much can I do?' I was quite shocked to find that I couldn't do very far before I had to come back - about a mile, if that, and it was really difficult getting back to the car and getting in it - that was another problem, getting in and out of the car with crutches. But over time I started going there once a week and after a while I managed to do the full trip, then I did the whole walk on one crutch and I substituted the crutch in the end for a stick, and then I had the stick for a long time.

Less than a year after the accident, I went in to the college for my leaving-do and then Rolly, who's head of English, invited me to a party he was having and at the party there was a lot of music and I decided I would dance and I did dance, so then I thought, why have I got this stick when I can dance? And that was when I gave up the stick. Then I went off to see my friend Pep in Barcelona and walked all over Barcelona.

But that was almost a year out of my life really, as a sculptor, it was certainly six months out of my life and of course I was due to retire on 31st January 2011, and I couldn't even get into college, so my farewell party was delayed and then delayed again.

In a funny sort of way it gave me a lot of time to think, first of all spending time with Linda looking back over my life, creating the archive website, and later these memoirs. But also it gave me a lot of time to think about what I wanted to do with my life from now on, and how I wanted to conduct myself, and what's amazed me is I've been so productive. I always was productive, on my days off, but I did have to teach three days a week, and I had to prepare, and all that took time, and then I had family.

I suppose the disappointment is that my family didn't really take it on board what had happened to me, I don't think, and that was a bit of a shock, specially with my daughter. But she'd just started a new relationship, she did live in London, but I was quite shocked that in a way she neglected me, and in a way some of it was my fault because I told her not to come down, because it was very icy, and the boyfriend was driving her down so for the two or three weeks when I first came out it was my fault that they didn't come down because I told them not to, but there wasn't that excuse all the time. We've talked about it since, and she said 'well you are very independent, I knew you'd be all right' but there was the psychological thing that I was dependent on my friends really psychologically and they were really good, so I had things to look forward to.

I'm surprised I wasn't depressed, I was quite optimistic about getting better. I was worried that I would have a limp, and about the bone density. When they first told me I'd got osteoporosis I came back home and I thought 'Shit! Will I ever make sculpture again?' Because I remembered Stephen, the boy Nigel and I helped in Lincolnshire who'd got osteoporosis. I was very worried till I said to Dr Vince 'should I be making sculpture, will I break a bone?' and he said 'no it's not that bad and actually you need a bit of vibration in your bones, so knocking your sculpture and doing that, that's good for it' and after that I wasn't so depressed.

Once I'd got a bit more mobile I started making the first acrylic figure, which is almost the same as the cardboard one, it's not quite the same stance because the material's a bit thicker than the cardboard. Where the waist is joined there are only two points that are actually stuck from the top half onto the bottom half, so there's not much holding it, and it's an incredible weight, in fact when I was putting it together to stick it, it slipped and I only just managed to catch it before the whole top half fell apart.

It's a different piece altogether because you can see through it, it's got transparencies on it, and they're not of paper like on the cardboard one, I've put some of the painted pieces on it and I think it's finished now as far as it's going. I'm not sure if I like it as much as the cardboard piece, but then that's often the case with sculpture, that something you like instantly when you've made it, a couple of months down the line you most probably think it's the worst thing you've done and sometimes if you make something and you think it's not that good, after a while you think it's really good. I've noticed this through my career, but I've only recently worked out how it happens. I think it's because of what the subconscious puts into the work without the conscious mind realising it. When it's first done, there's something there that the conscious mind doesn't recognise and doesn't like much. It has to take a while for that to percolate through and when that's happened, I appreciate the work more. But if I like a piece straight away, when time passes and I come back to look at it again, I'm disappointed, because it doesn't have that extra contribution, so it feels as though it didn't really stretch me. So I'm still waiting to see the evaluation of the acrylic dancer.

My friend Richard came and gave me a critique of it when he was over from France and I found that helpful, and at the start of 2012 I started making another one. This one's different because this is all material that I got free from Barlo International when I was in Barcelona. I don't know whether they gave it to me because it had a problem but on one side it's got a white plastic backing to protect it and on the other side it's got a blue plastic backing. The blue plastic backing peels off easily, but the white plastic backing doesn't, obviously it did at one time but now it's sort of stuck and the only way you can get it off is to use a steamer, the sort that you use to get wallpaper off, and then use a spatula and scrape it off that way. It still leaves the gluey stuff on that they stuck the plastic on with, so I then have to clean it up with white spirit and get it all off, so it's quite a process. Then I had to laminate the photocopies on by using a sort of transfer method, so now I'm making another figure with the white left on because it's got some interesting lines going through it which is caused by the white plastic backing shrinking.

It was always my intention to make two anyway, so when I took the cardboard one apart, because I had to take the cardboard one apart to make a template of the shapes to reproduce them in acrylic, I actually did two versions of everything. So all the white one's cut out, I've just now got to stick it together and I'm going to change bits of it, I've already started changing

185

little bits of it, so it'll be another completely new piece. And now I've stuck the cardboard one back together again because everybody was so dismayed - for some reason people really do like the cardboard one. I mean, I like it, it's very sort of in a way cubistic and it's made me think about work that I'm going to do in the future because I think that I'm coming to an end of doing these very colourful pieces and I'd quite like to have time to digest what I've been doing in the last year since my accident and then think about what I'm going to make in the future.

This mustn't be taken too seriously, because I often change my mind, but I've got a feeling that I'd like to make some other figurative pieces, maybe in a different material altogether. One of the things that I actually wanted to do was to make the figure in bronze plate all welded up because then it could go outside. I think it's quite an interesting figure, but then in bronze it wouldn't have all the patterns so I don't know - this white one won't have anywhere near the amount of patterns because it's just where the plastic bit has pulled apart, so it'll be interesting to see what it looks like.

Most of it is just done as experimentation, all the work is done as just experimenting, I arrived at doing the *Codices* and *Table for One* and all the ones that I think are important that sort of way.

Now I'm going to think about trying to get an exhibition, I've got to do that for myself and also to find out what's going to happen to my work if and when I die because I'm very worried at the moment that it will all just suddenly disappear if I'm not careful so I'm trying to get in contact with people. It's just getting myself around and meeting people, which I don't do enough of, I'm inclined to cut myself off in the workshop and I think that's the nature of being a sculptor, if you work with the material. There's two ways of making sculpture, you either come up with an idea and then find the material to fit the idea or you play with the material and get an idea out of the material, so there are always two different ways of creating sculpture, and I think I use both of them.

Because of the way I was brought up, and all the people I knew who were like my history, my grandfather and great grandfather who were pastry cooks making things with their hands and my father and his father who were bricklayers, I've always felt that I've got to be physically active. It's only just dawned on me recently that at times when I think I'm being lazy my mind is ticking away like mad, because normally when I think I'm not doing anything I'm drawing, but I've also realised that there are times when I'm not drawing or making art at all but I'm still thinking about my sculpture.

When I was in France this year (2011) a friend of mine said 'what have you been doing?' and I said 'actually I've been thinking about my work' and then it dawned on me that there's all this sort of mental activity that takes over: 'What am I going to do when I go back? How is this going to affect that?' I've always had this sort of work ethic where I think I've got to work at least six hours a day on my sculpture, and I get very frustrated if I can't, like yesterday I had to spend the day with the accountant and I had to go to Cambridge and get other things that I needed for the house, and I spent all the bloody day yesterday on that, apart from I did manage to do some transferring of these images. I always get frustrated when that happens, I've got a lot of things I've put off which are going to take all day tomorrow too.

And it's so frustrating because I thought when I retired I'd have seven days to do my work but it's not worked out like that, I spend just as much time, not quite as much as teaching but I spend a lot of time doing things I don't really want to do like gardening - you know, I want the garden to look nice but I don't really want to do it, and just doing other activities, sorting out my pension, getting all this in order, trying to work out the text and the photographs and everything on the computer, I spent till about half past two last night on the computer just working, trying to send out letters, trying to do things to help get on professionally so I can make a living out of it, which I've never been able to do.

And it's just dawned on me that when I've got these if you like fallow times when I think I'm not doing anything and I'm just basically sitting in the garden it's not true, I'm actually working out what my priorities for a piece are. I remember when I was studying Zen Buddhism this idea of 'monkey-mind' because I often have more than one idea in my head and I'm thinking should I go along with that? At the moment I'm at this crisis where I'm still making abstract art but like I've done in the past, I keep thinking I ought to be making something much more figurative, something that people can get an idea about but also to represent the figurative in a very contemporary way, not to actually make like the torsos and things, things that you recognise as strictly figurative work but to actually transform the figurative in a new way, and that's what this figure is trying to do. So that's been quite important to me and I think that the last time I was in Łódź was quite important because out of that came the start of thinking about a much more figurative approach.

In January 2012 I met up with Gustav Metzger again, in Cambridge this time. I was rather shocked to see him, for a start he wasn't where he was supposed to be, I was supposed to meet him in the Ruskin Gallery at Anglia Ruskin University, and he was at an exhibition, quite an interesting exhibition put on in Regent Street, in Cambridge. I mentioned earlier about the city council's project to use empty shops for short exhibitions, we met at one of these things, only it wasn't students, it was two artists from London, so this was quite a professional show but it was in an old shop in a prominent part of Cambridge. I was quite pleased that things had gone so far and that there was a certain sort of professionalism taking over. Because students' work can vary, it can be very good or it can be poor and you are putting it in the public domain, so I feel a tiny bit responsible for that happening.

It was nice to meet Gustav there, but I was so shocked when I met him because when I'd met him in Barcelona in 1999 at the private view of the *Action* exhibition at the MACBA, he bounded over to me, I recognised him and he recognised me, he looked exactly the same as I'd remembered from over 30 years before. We'd talked about when he did the auto-destructive art at the Hayward Gallery, and I remember him coming in to St Martin's and asking for volunteers from the students to help him, so I knew it had to have been when I was studying there, and it was rather a shock when I met him again in 2012 and he said 'no it didn't happen between 1962 and 1965 it happened in 1961'. I can't see how it could happen in 1961 because I wasn't at St Martin's in 1961 so somewhere somebody's got their dates wrong or I've misinterpreted what he said to me

I was rather astounded to be faced with somebody I didn't recognise, and he was quite doubled over compared to what he was in 1999. I know he's 85 but I've never seen quite such deterioration in somebody in 12 years. I think his mind's all there - he's obviously got a problem with dates, but it made me realise that maybe I have too, but I know I met him between 1962 and 1965 because there's no way I would have known him when I was at Croydon, so it definitely happened between 1962 and 1965. He said 'I came in and gave a lecture in 1965', and I find that hard to believe too, because I would have been working on my large sculpture and my final year exhibition, and also I was doing the Sainsbury award at the Tate, so I find it very hard to believe that I would have had time to go to a lecture, so I've got an idea that he came in 1964.

He made me aware not only of my own fragility and the fact that I'm getting older, but also that you do lose track of dates and times and events and when you did things, and I think that's an important thing with something like these memoirs because I'm going to have to check things, it is difficult to keep a track of everything. And I started asking him questions, questions that always interested me that I never had time to ask him.

So it was quite important to meet Gustav but I was shocked how much he'd aged and I found it rather sad really because when you've been at the centre of things like Gustav has, I don't know how much the nation really appreciates people like that. All the time I've known him he spent his life destroying his works of art, auto-destructive art as he called it, so he was in league with people like Tinguely the French sculptor who used to make these machines that fell apart and Niki de Saint Phalle who used to shoot paintings and sculpture and things, he comes from that sort of ideas background. I'm hoping that he will get his way and he will get a foundation because there is always the problem of what you do with your work.

The friend who brought him to Cambridge had taken him to see Wittgenstein's grave in Cambridge and I assumed that he'd been to Cambridge University and that he'd had something to do with Wittgenstein, but he said to me, no, the reading of Wittgenstein was much later after the 1960s. Then he told me that he'd gone to Cambridge School of Art and actually he'd enrolled to do life drawing and that was a bit of a shock. So maybe he's got some life drawings left somewhere, as I have.

I was rather disappointed there wasn't a photograph taken of me and him because I would have liked it for my own records, not for publicity or anything, I mean he is looking exceptionally frail and I have got fond memories of him, he was a really nice person and he said that students were much more questioning and rebellious in the 1950s, well I couldn't actually agree with that, but then perhaps our histories have been different.

So although we disagreed about dates, Gustav and I, we ended on the note that we'd meet again. And I was rather disappointed that I'd missed a

Editor's Postscript

In January 2012, while we were working together on this book, Douglas Jeal was diagnosed with motor neurone disease, and sadly passed away in 2015.

After his diagnosis, we continued editing the book together, and I think neither of us really wanted to face up to writing an additional chapter about his diagnosis and illness.

Douglas saw proof copies, helped with proof reading and was happy with the text and layout as it stands, but wanted to include pictures of his life and work. Although this would have greatly increased the production costs, we discussed colour illustrations, and he was planning to source them. However, during the last year of his life, we had very little contact, partly due to his illness, but also because I was taken ill in the autumn of 2014, and when I recovered, moved to the south coast. Consequently, I never received any illustrations from him, although pictures of his work prior to 2011 can be found on his website, www.douglasjeal.com.

I have thought long and hard about what to do with this book. It seems to me that, even without the illustrations, it is better to leave it as it is, with the text and layout that Douglas saw and was happy with. So, I am publishing it as it stands, as my tribute to Douglas, a talented and innovative artist, and a dear friend.

Linda Rushby,
Southsea, Hampshire, July 2017

retrospective exhibition of him a couple of years ago, I don't know how I'd missed it perhaps I was in Poland or something, so that annoyed me a bit, but then you can't keep up with everything.

I had another encounter that made me think towards the end of 2011. I've known Pep and his first wife Nuri since 1987, I used to go out and see them in Barcelona three times a year, and I've lived out there, of course, a couple of times, so I used to see a lot of them. Then when they broke up, I still used to see Nuri because they stayed friendly and they've got a daughter just a bit younger than Angie. But when I went to visit Pep before Christmas 2011 he said, 'I didn't want to tell you over the phone because I haven't seen you for three years, but Nuri died two and a half years ago' and I said, 'well, I didn't know she was ill' and he said she died of cancer really quickly. I hadn't realised, because I forgot about me being out of action for so long after the accident, that it was so long since I'd been over there. Pep and Nuri were younger than me, when I got to know them they were in their twenties and I was in my forties, so Nuri could only have been about 47, and their poor daughter was only 17 at the time. She was all right but it's obviously affected her to lose your mum at 17.

Pep said to me, 'd'you know, you're the oldest - the longest-standing friend I've got left', and he is with me, I mean so many other people I've known have died off, it's quite frightening really. So it was quite emotional going out there, it was good and I did some drawing in a park, and now I've started drawing again. As I've said before, I have periods in my life when I draw and periods when I don't and I started drawing - I quite like drawing parks and spaces and people sitting on benches and trees, because you have to portray the distance and relationships to form and space in a drawing. So I started drawing again, I lost one of my little black notebooks, but it was quite an emotional time and it was really good to be in Barcelona again.

www.ingramcontent.com/pod-product-compliance
Lightning Source LLC
La Vergne TN
LVHW051630080426
835511LV00016B/2268